China's Catholics

Map 1. China: provinces and major cities.

Comparative Studies in Religion and Society
Mark Juergensmeyer, editor

China's Catholics

Tragedy and Hope in an
Emerging Civil Society

Richard Madsen

UNIVERSITY OF CALIFORNIA PRESS
Berkeley · Los Angeles · London

University of California Press
Berkeley and Los Angeles, California

University of California Press, Ltd.
London, England

© 1998 by
The Regents of the University of California

Library of Congress Cataloging-in-Publication Data

Madsen, Richard, 1941–
    China's Catholics : tragedy and hope in an
emerging civil society / Richard Madsen.
        p.   cm. — (Comparative studies in religion and society; 12)
    Includes bibliographical references and index.
    ISBN 0-520-21326-2 (alk. paper)
        1. Catholic Church—China.   I. Title.
BX1665.M29   1999
282'.51'09045—dc21   97-50613

Printed in the United States of America
9 8 7 6 5 4 3 2 1

Contents

Illustrations

PHOTOGRAPHS

MAPS

Acknowledgments

When I left the Maryknoll Fathers in the early 1970s, I promised my colleagues and myself that I would one day use my academic training to help them better understand the Catholic Church in China. An opportunity to fulfill that promise came through funding granted by the Luce Foundation in its program to encourage collaboration between American and Chinese scholars. I am grateful to Terrill Lautz of the Luce Foundation not only for providing the funding but also for his wise advice and generous encouragement over many years.

For me the happiest and most fruitful part of the collaboration facilitated by the Luce Foundation was working with Fan Lizhu, who accompanied me in my fieldwork in Tianjin, carried out many of the interviews for this book, and has now written several papers in Chinese on this work. I also owe a large debt to her colleagues in the Tianjin Academy of Social Sciences who also participated in our Luce project—especially Wang Hui, the president of the Academy, Li Shiyu, Pan Yunkang, Li Baoliang, Hua Qingzhao, and Dong Huifan. My American collaborators in the Luce project were Susan Shirk, David Jordan, Linton Freedman, Ruan Danqing, Christopher Nevitt, Joseph Esherick, and Paul Pickowitz. I am grateful for their friendship and intellectual stimulation.

In working on this book, I also received an immense amount of help from old and dear friends in the Catholic Church who have spent much of their lives studying about China, especially Fr. Peter Barry, MM;

Sr. Janet Carroll, MM; Fr. Edward Malatesta, S.J.; Fr. Michel Masson, S.J.; and Jean-Paul Wiest.

A grant from the University of California, San Diego, Academic Senate enabled me to travel to Taiwan and Hong Kong to gather information important to this book. And A-chin Hsiau was an energetic and effective research assistant.

My colleagues Robert Bellah, William Sullivan, Ann Swidler, and Steven Tipton read much of the manuscript and helped me to clarify some important theoretical points. Mark Juergensmeyer encouraged me to bring the manuscript to the University of California Press. Pamela Fischer contributed excellent copyediting. None of these people, of course, are in any way responsible for whatever errors of interpretation I have made on this controversial topic.

As always, my wife, Judy Rosselli, and my daughter, Susan, gave me abundant inspiration and support.

Finally, I would like to dedicate this book to Donald MacInnis, who more than a quarter of a century ago inspired and encouraged me to undertake the academic study of Christianity in its Chinese context and who has long provided a role model to emulate.

Note on Romanization

In this book, I use the pinyin form of Romanization when rendering words used in the People's Republic of China. However, when rendering proper names of people or places located in Taiwan, I use the Wade-Giles Romanization, which is in common use there. When rendering proper names of Chinese people in the United States and Europe, I use the Romanization that they or their organizations commonly use. For instance, the family name of the cardinal of Shanghai is Cardinal Gong in pinyin Romanization, and I refer to him in that way when speaking of his life in mainland China. In the United States, however, he and his foundation refer to him as Cardinal Kung, which is the form of Romanization now used mostly in Taiwan. When referring to the activities of his foundation in the United States, I call it the Cardinal Kung Foundation, which is the way a reader will find it in directories used in this country.

Introduction

The Context of Chinese Catholicism

Early in the morning of August 15, 1992, I attended a Mass celebrating the Feast of the Assumption of Mary at St. Joseph's Cathedral (also known as Old Xikai Cathedral) in the northern Chinese coastal city of Tianjin. The Assumption is one of the "four great feast days" in the Chinese Catholic liturgical year (the other three being Christmas, Easter, and Pentecost), and the Catholics in Tianjin celebrated it accordingly. Even though August 15 fell on a Saturday, at the time a workday in China, the cathedral was packed to its thousand-person capacity for the 7:30 A.M. Mass;[1] every seat was taken, and no standing room was left in the aisles. The participants were roughly equally divided between women and men (women only slightly in the majority), and about half the participants seemed to be younger than forty. The new bishop of Tianjin, Bishop Shi Hongchen, presided over a glorious solemn high Mass, with a degree of pomp and grandeur rarely seen in the West since the second Vatican Council of the mid-1960s. The bishop was assisted by a dozen altar boys (middle-school-aged, clad in red cassocks, with white and blue surplices) plus a full array of acolytes and deacons. Three stately processions occurred during different parts of the ceremonies; these processions were grand displays of hierarchical order: a cross bearer, row upon row of candle bearers, a deacon swinging a censer, the bishop with his miter and crosier followed by a half dozen other attendants. Each of the ministers wore a vestment appropriate to his station, the most spectacular being that of the bishop, who wore a red robe with a ten-foot-long train, which was held up in the back by an acolyte.

Included in the ceremonies was the First Communion of more than a hundred children, most in the fourth and fifth grades, who had spent their summer vacation attending daily classes at the church in preparation for the event (despite government regulations forbidding religious instruction to persons under eighteen). The boys wore red cassocks, and the girls long white dresses with crowns of artificial red flowers on their heads. In the opening procession, the First Communion recipients each carried long-stemmed gladiolus; they solemnly placed these flowers in large vases on the ornate main altar, which was ablaze with candles and lights.

The behavior of the worshipers was in keeping with the splendor of the liturgy. Mostly dressed in their best clothes, men sitting on the left and women on the right side of the cathedral, the worshipers knelt and bowed in unison with what by American Catholic standards seemed like extraordinary attentiveness and devotion. Although the bishop and his ministers said the prayers of the Mass in Latin in virtually inaudible voices with their backs to the people, pre–Vatican II style, the worshipers in the pews participated enthusiastically in the liturgy by singing along with a twenty-person choir accompanied by an organ. The singing continued almost uninterrupted from the beginning to the end of the Mass. Most of the hymns were in Chinese, although there were some old Latin favorites like "Ave Maria." The singing was joyous, even triumphant, especially the opening processional, which was sung to the melody of the French national anthem. The thick stone wall of the church reverberated with the music.[2]

I was taken aback by the power and glory of the ceremony. I had been studying about the Chinese Catholic Church off and on for more than twenty years. My first trip to the People's Republic of China, in 1979, was with a tour of Protestant and Catholic church workers investigating the religious situation in China. As part of that tour, I attended a Sunday Mass in Guangzhou. I found it a somewhat depressing affair. Only a handful of worshipers, mostly elderly women, constituted a small and feeble congregation in a dark, cavernous cathedral. Since then, the government's policy of religious repression has been relaxed. In 1985, I attended Mass in Shanghai, in the famous Jesuit Sacred Heart Cathedral at Zikawei. This time the church was perhaps half full. In 1988, I attended Mass on Christmas day at the main cathedral in Beijing. This time it was full, but the ceremonies seemed listless, devoid of energy.

Figure 1. First Communion on the Feast of the Assumption at St. Joseph's Cathedral, Tianjin. Photograph courtesy of Jean Charbonnier, *Guide to the Catholic Church in China.*

Now, in the early 1990s, in spite of new and bitter divisions in the Church and in spite of ominous new government restrictions against religious practice, the liturgy seemed exuberant and joyous.

The scene at the Tianjin cathedral was part of a larger wave of religious revival that has been sweeping across China. Church members and leaders had been severely persecuted during the Cultural Revolution; most religious leaders were imprisoned or killed; all temples, churches, and mosques were closed and many were destroyed; and all public professions of faith were severely punished. But religious practice of all kinds has not only revived but has spread and flourished since the "reform and opening" of the post-Mao era. In the early morning, Buddhist temples resound with the sonorous chanting of monks, and throughout the day they are visited by crowds of worshipers placing thousands of smoking incense sticks in huge bronze receptacles and performing obeisance before restored images of Bodhisattvas. On Friday evenings newly rebuilt mosques are filled with Islamic worshipers, who are becoming an increasingly well-organized voice in Chinese society. On Sundays, burgeoning congregations of Protestants—which increased as much as twentyfold from the early 1980s to the mid-1990s!—fill officially approved churches and unofficial "meeting points." And Catholics, whose numbers have increased from about three million in 1949 to about ten million today, crowd into churches or gather illegally for Mass in large open spaces or in the privacy of homes.[3] Meanwhile, folk religious practices—ranging from ancestor worship to shamanism to the organization of outlawed secret societies like the "Unity Way" *(yiguandao)*—flourish throughout the countryside.[4]

The spread of all this religiosity has confounded the expectations of most foreign social scientists who have studied China. Although anthropologists have documented widespread religious practice in Chinese communities in Taiwan and Hong Kong, most social scientists who studied mainland China did not imagine that religion would become an important factor in Chinese life after being so thoroughly suppressed during the Maoist era. The efflorescence of religion, in spite of its continued discouragement by the Chinese government, forces us to reconsider assumptions about the human need for faith and about the attractions of religious community. It also raises important issues about the significance of revived forms of religious solidarity for China's political future.

Though focusing on a small part of the Chinese religious scene, the Catholic Church, I hope to address some larger questions about the causes and significance of religious revival in China. Why does religious practice continue to be attractive, and what makes it more attractive in some contexts than in others? Do the forces of social solidarity generated by religious practice contain resources that might enable some Chinese to resist the power of the Communist state or to construct a new, more humane, even more democratic, political order (or to do both)? Or does religion contain the seeds of social fragmentation and discord? Will religion contribute to or impede economic modernization? These are questions important not just for China but for all countries in transformation from state socialism.

Of course, the Chinese Catholic Church is too small (no more than one percent of the Chinese population) and too idiosyncratic to provide general answers to these questions. But within its recent history the Catholic Church dramatically illustrates many of the constructive energies as well as the social and political tensions associated with all kinds of religious revival throughout China. Although different religions manifest different configurations of these energies and tensions, this study of Catholicism can at least suggest ways of understanding issues associated with these other religions. And since Western readers are likely to be more familiar with Catholic beliefs and rituals than with those of

Eastern religions, a study of the Chinese Catholic Church may be for them a more accessible introduction to issues raised by religious revival in China than would a study of other, more typically Asian religions.

Knowledge about the Catholic Church in the West, especially in a country like the United States, cannot, however, be applied straightforwardly to Catholicism in China. Prejudgments will be quickly contradicted by the realities of Catholic life in China, an experience that will thus quickly (more quickly than if one were studying a religion about which one knew too little to be surprised) push one to ask hard and potentially productive questions about why the Church in China is so different from the Church in the West.

Thus, although I had been raised a Catholic, studied in a Catholic seminary, and worked for several years as a Catholic (Maryknoll) missionary in Taiwan, I was immediately surprised by many aspects of that Mass on the Feast of the Assumption in Tianjin, and I continued to be surprised after several months of attendance at the church. I was surprised at the level of enthusiasm of the worshipers. In the gusto of their singing and in the raptness of their demeanor—not to mention their willingness to gladly spend two and a half hours in church early on a Saturday morning—they seemed more devout than most Catholic congregations I have known in the United States. And indeed they were considerably more devout than congregations in Taiwan, where churches are much better appointed and where there are no obstacles to religious practice. (As one member of the Tianjin congregation put it to me matter of factly, "You know, we Catholics in the Third World are a lot more devout than you in the First World.") Why does religion loom as a more important part of the lives of practicing Catholics in contemporary China than in the West?

And what are the social consequences of this importance? Although I initially found the Tianjin Catholics' devotion moving, I gradually became uneasy about it. There was obviously a great deal of constructive religious energy here. In the way in which the Tianjin Catholics had organized their beautiful singing, in the way in which parents had educated their children in preparation for First Communion, in the familiarity and affection with which the Catholics greeted one another after Mass, one could sense an inspiring capacity for cooperation based on mutual trust. But as they approached the communion rail to receive the Body of Christ, with hands reverently folded, I was taken aback to see how they pushed and jostled each other to get to the communion rail first. Intertwined with the religiously inspired capacity for cooperation,

Figure 2. Bishop Shi Hongchen. Photograph by Richard Madsen.

there was a harsh, perhaps even dangerous, competitiveness. And over the self-regulating order of life in Church, there was a coercive framework of power. As people approached the altar for Holy Communion, some were firmly turned away by ushers, who scrutinized each member of the congregation to see whether he or she belonged in the church.

Upon leaving the church, the members of the congregation milled around in little clusters, chatting amiably with their friends, perhaps checking out the announcements of upcoming events or sampling the religious literature placed on tables in the courtyard; superficially they appeared like a typical congregation in the United States. Yet I soon found that the sociability covered histories of tragedy and prospects of danger that one does not expect in the United States. This distinguished-looking man, chatting happily with his grandchildren, used to be a priest, renounced the priesthood under pressure from the Communists in the early 1950s, but nonetheless ended up being branded a rightist during the antirightist movement and spent twenty years in prison. That man over there is rumored to be a member of the secret police, sent to check on the political orthodoxy of the Catholics and perhaps even to undermine their community.

Then there is the underground Church. As I left the cathedral, on that Feast of the Assumption, some members warmly welcomed me and ushered me forward to take pictures of the first communicants and to

Figure 3. Our Lady of Lourdes grotto at the Tianjin cathedral, meeting place
for the underground Church. Photograph by Richard Madsen.

meet the bishop. They were especially eager that I have my picture
taken with Bishop Shi. It was not until over a year later, when I spent
several months in Tianjin continuing my research project, that I learned
why I had been welcomed so warmly. "You didn't realize it, but you
were a great help to us that day," said a friend of mine from the church.
"The underground Church was going to make a disturbance, but we
told them, 'Hold off, there's a foreigner here taking pictures.'" The disturbance was averted, and nothing marred the First Communion day of
the children from St. Joseph's Cathedral.

The underground Church consists of Catholics who refuse to accept
the regulations concerning public religious practice imposed by the Chinese government on the Church. The underground believed that Bishop
Shi had betrayed the faith by carrying out his ministry under terms set
by the government. "This is not a matter of private feelings or personal
ideas," said a pamphlet secretly distributed by the underground. "This
is a 'line question'—a question of whether one does or does not believe
in Jesus."[5] While Mass was going on inside the cathedral, a group of
more than a hundred underground Catholics knelt in the courtyard outside chanting the rosary in front of a statue of Our Lady of Lourdes.
They steadily raised the volume of their insistent chanting in competi-
tion with the loudspeakers aimed at them, which conveyed the Mass

taking place within the cathedral. Other underground Catholics stayed locked in their homes because of a rumor that on that Feast of the Assumption in 1992 the sky would darken and the world would end.

Clearly, the patterns of cooperation and conflict manifested in the Catholic Church in Tianjin are different from those in the United States. And the role of Catholicism—and indeed of religion in general—in Chinese society is different from its role in Western liberal democracies. In the chapters that follow, I will explain some of the reasons for these differences and spell out their implications not just for Catholics but for all those concerned about China's capacity to make a peaceful transition away from a rigid state socialism toward an open society.

CATHOLICISM AND CHINA'S SPIRITUAL CRISIS

The conflicted reemergence of the Catholic Church is one of many responses to a spiritual crisis facing China at the end of this century. A profound crisis of meaning indeed affects most societies in the world. Vaclav Havel puts it eloquently. "Today, many things indicate that we are going through a transitional period, when it seems that something is on the way out and something else is painfully being born. It is as if something were crumbling, decaying and exhausting itself, while something else, still indistinct, were arising from the rubble." Like other great moments of transition in human civilizations—the Renaissance, for example—this is a period, says Havel, "when all consistent value systems collapse, when cultures distant in time and space are discovered or rediscovered . . . New meaning is gradually born from the encounter, or the intersection, of many different elements."[6]

Although all cultures today are unhappy, each is unhappy in its own way. The crisis of meaning in contemporary China bears the marks of that society's particular, traumatic twentieth-century history. The century began, for China, with the collapse of the old empire and, in the era of the May Fourth Movement, with an iconoclastic rejection by China's leading intellectuals of the traditional cultural system that had sustained the old order.[7] Of course, similar rejections of traditional values, in the name of some combination of social revolution, anti-imperialist nationalism, and economic modernization, took place around the world. But China's rejection of tradition was particularly tumultuous and sweeping. The prolonged trauma of the Sino-Japanese war followed by a bloody civil war delayed the development of a new cultural synthesis. After the Chinese Communists won the civil war, they tried indeed to create a new, unified Chinese culture but in a way that only deepened the crisis.

Mao Zedong attempted to substitute a political ideology for traditional culture and to make himself the sole arbiter of that ideology's correctness. The result, as Jiwei Ci puts it, "was the building of morality on the most shifting of foundations. Political programs fail easily, and political beliefs sacrosanct today can look ridiculous tomorrow. People act on a politically grounded morality only when they subscribe to certain political beliefs, and these beliefs command allegiance only when the political program of which they are a part is thriving. It was thus a source of potential disaster that Mao's China relied on a political morality that could last only as long as Mao and his political program lasted." [8]

The disastrous potential was realized in the most cataclysmic way when Mao's politics led to the Cultural Revolution. In that event the Maoists destroyed their credibility by destroying the lives of millions of people. So after the death of Mao a whole generation of Chinese had to come to terms with, as the dissident filmmaker Su Xiaokang puts it, "life made abnormal by fanaticism, by passion, naiveté, blindness, frankness, and even dedication." The need to "redeem ourselves" from the misguided, destructive zeal of the Cultural Revolution is, says Su, a matter of what "philosophers call 'ultimate concerns.'" [9] Yet many of the cultural resources for dealing with these ultimate concerns had been obliterated by several generations of indoctrination in Maoist ideology.

Compared with most modern societies trying to find unifying meanings in times of transition, then, China's people today have ready access to fewer traditional cultural resources and must confront a recent past that poses excruciating questions. At the same time, explosive economic growth creates inequalities, forces dislocations, and engenders corruption—in short, poses urgent moral and political questions.

Under these circumstances, many people in China are earnestly searching for meaning and are renewing their affiliation with communities that carry such meaning. The revival of Catholicism is one small part of this. But it remains to be seen whether such quests will be conducive to public order or will improve Chinese society. Thirty years of isolation from the outside world—from the founding of the People's Republic of China in 1949 to the beginning of Deng Xiaoping's new policy of "reform and opening" in 1978—and almost fifty years of systematic indoctrination in socialist ideology have not led to a widespread belief in that political ideology, but they have inhibited the development of other forms of belief. When, for example, Catholics try to find in their theology a guide to a good life in an ideologically devastated landscape, they have, in many cases, only shaky memories of an outdated theology. Often these shaky memories are of just those parts of the doctrine that have enabled small communities to hunker down against hostile attacks from outsiders, not those parts that would encourage ecumenical cooperation with a wide variety of outsiders. At the same time, many other groups—Protestants, Buddhists, Daoists, Muslims, practitioners of all sorts of folk religion, as well as intellectuals searching for secular answers to "ultimate concerns"—are engaged in their own confused spiritual quests, which sometimes emphasize the more rigid, exclusive parts of their traditions. The result of such a religious revival could easily be the breakdown of society into conflicting segments rather than the creation of a new public culture—"new meaning . . . from the encounter, or the intersection, of many different elements"—that could provide a constructive, common framework for a complex, diverse society.

China's spiritual crisis thus has potentially important consequences for China's social and political development. At stake is whether and how China might develop a "civil society" composed of relatively autonomous communities that could mitigate the harshness of an unregulated market economy, protect citizens from the oppression of a tyrannical regime, and facilitate the establishment of responsible self-governance. It is on these social and political consequences of China's Catholic revival—and, by suggestion, the revival of other forms of religion—that I will focus in this book.

There are other extremely interesting and important dimensions of the Catholic response to China's spiritual crisis, dimensions that might be central for sociologists of religion or for theologians and Catholic Church authorities. Instead of the social consequences of Chinese Catholicism, for instance, one might concentrate on the phenomenology of the Catholic religious experience itself and give a sense of what it feels like to maintain a faith in an almighty, benevolent God in the face of the most terrible and seemingly senseless suffering. Or one might discuss with more subtlety than I have managed here the ways in which Catholic communities are reinterpreting their traditional doctrine in light of changing circumstances and in light of new knowledge about changes in Catholicism from the universal Church. Or one might analyze the patterns of reasoning that Catholics use in applying their moral principles to the dilemmas of ordinary life.[10] I hope that this work of mine might someday encourage other scholars to pursue these lines of research. For now, however, I myself simply do not have the richness of data necessary to pursue them. And, in the meantime, the question of the development of what some scholars call a civil society in China is one of the most urgent and important questions facing the world today.

THE PROBLEM OF CIVIL SOCIETY

What exactly is meant by "civil society"? Generally, the term refers to self-governed associations through which citizens can participate in an organized way in public affairs. The term has come back into vogue both as the carrier of earnest political hopes and as an analytic tool for guiding intellectuals toward a realization of those hopes.[11] Normatively, civil society refers to what Ernest Gellner calls "the conditions of liberty"—that is, the conditions for democratic citizenship.[12] Civil society was used as a rallying cry by dissidents in Eastern Europe in their discussions about how state socialism could be replaced by democracy. It is used by Western social theorists in their discussions about how the democratic ideal might be institutionalized in mass societies with apathetic publics dominated by corporate capitalism and bureaucratic states. It is used by would-be revolutionaries in the Third World in their rhetoric about breaking free of the hegemony of global capitalism.

Behind all these disparate discussions is a search for a society in which all citizens can play an active, even if indirect and partial, role in forging a consensus about the rules by which they will be governed. Though a product of the Western Enlightenment, this sense that it is an essential part of human dignity that each citizen have some voice in governance is now widely shared throughout most of the world. There is, of course, no consensus about how to realize this ideal. It is indeed becoming apparent that simply importing the formal institutions of liberal democracy—multiparty political systems, constitutional checks and balances, even free elections—into countries that are bitterly divided along lines of social class, ethnicity, religion, or region will not necessarily lead to a meaningful form of democracy. For instance, as William Sullivan has put it, "in some nations newly emerging from authoritarian regimes. . . , the rush to elections may be actually weakening the new states, creating a problem of stability while undermining the legitimacy of democracy in the eyes of their citizens."[13] And in spite of its formally free institutions, some critics would say, the United States is becoming less an effective democracy and more an oligarchy controlled by wealthy corporate interests.[14]

Democracy is an ideal that can never be perfectly realized. But if it is to be even partially achieved, it would seem to require a certain social capacity for self-governance. People have to be able to participate in groups through which they can articulate and if necessary defend their interests. Analytically, then, civil society refers to the associations through which they can do so. But are all the self-governing groups that citizens use to pursue and protect their interests to be considered a part of civil society? To push this argument to the extreme, should terrorist groups be considered part of civil society? Insofar as the analytic use of civil society is aimed at the normative goal of determining the conditions for the (partial, inevitably imperfect) realization of democratic ideals, it should be capable of distinguishing between those groups that are conducive to social self-governance and those that are not.[15]

Unfortunately, much discussion of civil society does not make these distinctions. For instance, in 1996 in an article in the *Washington Post* with the headline "Fragile Civil Society Takes Root in Chinese Reform," Steven Mufson wrote, "The Communist Party still rules supreme, but its tentacles no longer reach into every nook and cranny of life. Independent filmmakers, underground churches, private businesses, antismoking groups, private schools, foundations, think tanks, women's support groups, art salons, stamp clubs—such organizations have bubbled up and in their own ways are testing the limits of Communist control. About 200,000 groups have registered with the Civil Affairs Ministry; thousands more operate informally."[16] Like good journalism, this article reflects the views of a wide range of experts who have been writing about Chinese civil society. It also reflects the inconsistencies and confusions found within this spectrum. Are underground churches, private businesses, antismoking groups, stamp clubs, and the "2000 peasant societies of all descriptions" in Liaoning Province (mentioned in another part of the article) all conducive to social self-governance? Should they all be seen as part of a civil society?

My study of the Catholic Church was part of a larger interdisciplinary project sponsored by the Luce Foundation to build a theoretical and empirical foundation for answering such questions. In addition to this book, that larger project funded three other collaborative projects that brought together scholars from the University of California, San Diego, the University of California, Irvine, and the Tianjin Academy of

Social Sciences. The topics of the subprojects ranged from associations of entrepreneurs to organizations of marriage brokers to networks of family and friends.[17] Though they employed different methodologies and different theoretical frameworks, they each contributed to a complex dialogue about whether a civil society was emerging in contemporary China and what its prospects for the future were. This dialogue took the form of many hours of discussion among members of the project, culminating in a three-day conference in June 1993. In the remainder of this chapter, I will briefly recount how the questions raised in this book were shaped by this larger dialogue. In Chapter 5, I will show how the answers to those questions have contributed to the dialogue funded by the Luce Foundation and how it, in turn, might contribute to wider dialogues about civil society.

Like most discussion of civil society among China scholars in the early 1990s, our dialogue initially focused on the degree of independence from the state a group would have to have to function as a part of a civil society. Inevitably, from this point of view, China does not seem to have the basis for much of a civil society. In China, the government forbids the constitution of independent groups. Indeed, the main demand of the protesters whose movement was crushed around Tiananmen Square in 1989 was to be allowed to constitute such organizations, particularly autonomous student associations and labor unions. If, however, one takes a point of view that does not focus so exclusively on the formal independence of social groups, one might have reason for more optimism about civil society in China. Many groups that are formally connected to the government apparatus are, as the sociologist Ding Xueliang has put it, "amphibious"—they are not confined to life within the state-controlled environment, and they can develop their own agendas in at least partial independence from the state. Thus, in a situation characterized by "uncertainty, ambiguity, opacity, and confusion," a civil society may be forming under the carapace of the state.[18]

Much of the debate among Western scholars of China has been about how to tell whether a group has enough independence to be a constituent of a nascent civil society. Under conditions of "opacity" and "confusion," it is by definition difficult to gather sufficient evidence to answer such a question. Moreover, under conditions of "uncertainty" and "ambiguity" the evidence that one does obtain will be interpreted differently by people with different visions of the proper relation between citizens and the state in a modern society. Americans, for instance, tend to emphasize the need for maximum independence from government, while

Europeans tend to emphasize the need for a dynamic partnership between citizens and government. In my view, the combination of empirical confusion and theoretical debate has sapped much of the productiv-
ity out of recent discussions about civil society in China.

Thus, although the members of our Luce project initially focused on
how "civilian" various new forms of social organization emerging in
China during the Deng Xiaoping era were, I eventually decided to side-
step this debate and to focus instead on how much "civility" these forms
of organization manifested. To be part of the "conditions of liberty" not
only does a group have to be civilian—at least partially independent
and self-governing—it also has to have civility—it needs to embody
and sustain certain kinds of moral relationships.

In his study of what makes democracy work in Northern Italy,
Robert Putnam enumerates some of the main characteristics of such
relationships of civility. A first characteristic is civic engagement: the
members must be "alive to the interests of others." A second characteristic is a predominance of "horizontal relationships of reciprocity and
cooperation" over "vertical relationships of authority and dependence."
A third is high levels of solidarity, trust, and tolerance. A fourth characteristic is openness to involvement with different, overlapping associations, which moderates and expands loyalties and interests.[19]

To evaluate how much civility a group has, we must pay at least as
much attention to such moral characteristics as to the group's formal
status within the society. An association that is formally self-governing,
say, in the United States may in fact be riddled with dissension, or its
members may be apathetic or so narrow-minded that they have no concern for anyone outside the group. However, an organization in China
that is formally subordinated to a government agency and whose leaders can be chosen only with the approval of the Communist Party can in
fact have a great deal of actual autonomy. Its members may be deeply
committed to one another and determined to pursue their common
goals in spite of interference from the Party, and they may be deeply
committed to exerting some peaceful, constructive influence on public
affairs. A group like the Chinese one might be considered part of a cres-
cent civil society; the U.S. association might be an example of part of a
declining civil society.

In pluralistic societies such as the United States and for that matter in
much of Asia—as in Taiwan, Hong Kong, South Korea, and Japan—
the Catholic Church has for the most part played a constructive role in
fostering relations of civility. The same cannot necessarily be said of the

Catholic Church in China. Although from a theological point of view, it is the same as its sister Churches, it is sociologically different, with different practical understandings of the meaning of faith, the nature of authority, and the constitution of moral order. Often, the relationships fostered by the Chinese Catholic Church are just the opposite of those specified by Putnam: vertical rather than horizontal relationships; mistrust and belligerence rather than trust and tolerance; a contraction rather than an expansion of loyalties and interests.

This lack of civility is not in any straightforward way the result of the Church's lack of independence from the government. Like all other forms of religious organization in China, the Catholic Church is not permitted to function independently of a government-controlled "patriotic association." Obeying a higher authority, however, some defiant Catholics have set up illegal Church organizations, for which they can be severely punished if caught. Sometimes, however, these completely "civilian," illegal church organizations have less civility than those that operate legally, under the auspices of government-controlled organizations.

As we shall see, the Chinese Catholic Church has these characteristics because of the way in which its Counter Reformation theology and ecclesiastical authority structures have interacted in different contexts with Chinese culture, Chinese social structure, and the Chinese Communist state. Using ethnographic methods, I will attempt a "thick description" of what these uncivil characteristics look like in practice, and I will provide a brief account of how they came into being. Then I will explain why the Chinese Catholic Church has these features, at least in some Chinese contexts, and I will use this explanation to shed light on the general prospects for the development of civil society in China.

"CATHOLICS ARE NOTHING BUT TROUBLE": FIELDWORK IN CHINA

To determine the quality of the moral commitments that give groups such as the Chinese Catholic Church their vision and their strength requires ethnographic research. Some excellent books discuss the interaction between ecclesiastical authorities and the Chinese government, and I have made full use of them in this study. But relatively little is known about the beliefs and practices of ordinary Catholics, a kind of knowledge necessary to estimate the Church's potential for civility. To begin to get this knowledge, I carried out fieldwork in Tianjin. I chose Tianjin because of an accident of institutional affiliation. My university had established a productive cooperative relationship with the Tianjin Academy of Social Sciences that culminated in a successful joint application for a grant from the Luce Foundation. However, the region around Tianjin has the greatest concentration of Catholics in China, and it has produced some of the strongest conflicts between the underground and public churches and between Catholics and the government. It is the best place to get a comprehensive picture of both the hopeful and the troubling aspects of the Catholic Church in China.

Because of the conflicts in the Church in this region, fieldwork was extraordinarily difficult. When I arrived in Tianjin in 1992 for a two-week stay to lay the groundwork for my project, my colleagues at the Tianjin Academy of Social Sciences sought permission from the municipal Religious Affairs Bureau and other official agencies. My request was flatly denied. The official reason given was that the subject was "too sensitive." Less euphemistically, someone in the Religious Affairs Bureau told an acquaintance, "These Catholics are nothing but trouble. We don't give them any respect." According to the official orders, I was not to talk with any Catholics, especially not with any priests. This proscription was embarrassing to the Tianjin Academy of Social Sciences, which had approved my project as part of a package with the other three projects sponsored by the Luce Foundation, but they could not contravene the Religious Affairs Bureau's decision. I was, however, able to get permission to attend services on the Feast of the Assumption in order to observe and take pictures, as long as I did "not talk to any people at the church."

I went to the church in an official car accompanied by several people from the Academy. After the service, as I have recounted, some of the church people were extremely friendly because of their desire to use me as a buffer between themselves and the underground Church. They introduced me to the bishop and to several priests, although I did no more than exchange greetings with them. The following day was a Sunday. Members of the Tianjin Academy of Social Sciences had the day off, and I was left to relax and fend for myself. I took a cab to the cathedral for the 7:30 morning Mass. It was almost as crowded as on the Feast of the Assumption. (There are now four Masses every Sunday, and for each the cathedral is filled to capacity.) After the Mass, I was greeted by several people who had seen me the day before. One of them had been videotaping the ceremonies. He was going to show the videos to parents of the children who had received their First Communion, he said. Would I like to watch? So I went into the rectory and sat with a group of proud parents watching the tapes (which gave me a much better view of the ceremonies than I recorded with my own camera). The man with the video camera was a worker at the church who had also taken many photos of church events over the past several years. He showed me his photo album and gave me an informative account of the church's recent history. He also introduced me to several priests at the cathedral. I spent most of the day at the church, but I did not tell my colleagues at the Tianjin Academy of Social Sciences. If I had gotten into trouble, they would not be held responsible. I did not get into trouble (and neither did any of those who offered me their hospitality at the church). When I left China, the members of the Academy of Social Sciences were apologetic about their failure to gain permission for me to do research on the Catholic Church and promised to secure permission before my next visit, a two-month research trip in the fall of 1993.

For this two-month research stay, a colleague was assigned to me from the Academy of Social Sciences (in accordance with the Luce Foundation's stipulation that our research be collaborative). Fan Lizhu is a historian who has written several books about popular religion in China. She was an energetic fieldworker, a careful scholar, and a good friend. The information I have on the daily lives of Catholics is to a great extent the result of her hard work and initiative.

We were still not allowed to do any fieldwork on Catholics within Tianjin city. But we were allowed to make several investigations of "popular customs" in villages in the suburban counties of Tianjin. As I will explain in detail below, China's Catholics live mostly in the countryside, clustered together in villages that are almost entirely Catholic. We asked to study popular customs in villages that happened to be Catholic. We took several productive field trips to villages in Tianjin's suburban counties. After our initial trip, when we had to go with an entourage from the county seat, we traveled on our own by bus and bicycle and were warmly welcomed by most Catholic villagers we met. Eventually, however, the public security bureau got wind of our presence and made us stop "for your own protection."

Later, we traveled to Cangzhou, in Hebei Province, the center of a prefecture that has one of the highest concentrations of Catholics in China. Although the officials there were polite to us, they firmly forbade us to go to any of the places where the Catholics lived. They made us stay in our hotel, where they sent people to brief us on the official version of local history. However, between briefings we walked to the

Cangzhou Catholic church, where we again had some warm and informative conversations with the local priest and his congregation.

Another way we found to get around the limitations of access to Catholic villages was to interview people from the villages who now lived in the city. When we were in the villages, we were given names of people who had moved to Tianjin. We met them in their houses, usually small, cramped, dimly lit apartments off side streets or narrow alleys; theirs were not the houses of intellectuals or officials or budding entrepreneurs that most foreign visitors see in China. Often these transplants to the city gave us a more comprehensive, more articulate account of affairs in their home villages than we received from the people who still lived there.

Finally, although I was officially forbidden to do any research on the Catholic Church in Tianjin city, I went to Mass every Sunday at the cathedral and made a number of friends there, from whom I informally learned a great deal about Church affairs in the city.

By the time I left China, Fan Lizhu had become thoroughly familiar with the goals of the project. After I was gone, she took several trips by herself to Xian County in Cangzhou Prefecture, where she recorded interviews. She also returned to Baodi County and did the same. When, as part of the Luce Foundation project, she visited my university in San Diego, she brought the tapes of her interviews. I listened to them with her and with her help translated and transcribed them. Because language was no barrier for her and because of her warmth, openness, and empathy, the people she interviewed were often extraordinarily candid and colorful in speech.

All this is to say that this research was conducted under less than ideal conditions and presented serious practical and ethical difficulties. Because we did not have official permission for much of the research, we were not able to interview as many people as we would have liked. (Usually accompanied by Fan Lizhu, I interviewed about fifteen people—in interviews lasting from a half hour to three hours—in the Tianjin rural suburbs and in Tianjin city. On her own, Fan Lizhu interviewed about thirty in Xian County and seventeen in the Tianjin suburbs. Some of the suburban interviews were follow-ups of the same people we had interviewed during my stay in China.) But we saw a side of Chinese society that is normally kept from the view of outsiders. And by cross-checking accounts of people from different villages, by comparing the accounts of village residents with those of villagers who had moved to the city, and by comparing the accounts of long-time rural residents with the accounts of peasants, we were, I think, able to gain a reasonably comprehensive view of this hidden side of Chinese society. Ethical considerations led me to place some further limitations on my analysis. The topic of the underground Church was simply too sensitive to explore systematically without risking harm to our informants and trouble for my colleagues at the Tianjin Academy of Social Sciences. Therefore, most of what I say about the underground Church in this book is based on interviewing and documentary research done on my own, after the Tianjin portion of the research project had ended.

My information came mostly from Church workers in Hong Kong who travel frequently to visit Catholics in China. Some of them were trained journalists, who carry out their work with professional standards of objectivity. Others were concerned with providing pastoral care and financial aid to the Chinese; their reports were colored by their sense of mission. Still others were partisans of one or another faction within the Church. I tried to filter out biases by cross-checking reports of people representing different positions and by comparing the reports with my own ethnographic observations. Also, because of the sensitivity of this research topic, I have taken special care to conceal the names of people whom we interviewed. Sometimes, the cost is a lack of specificity about their exact living situations.

The interpretation of written documents posed similar problems to those of the oral interviews in Hong Kong. Numerous Catholic study centers in Hong Kong, Singapore, France, Belgium, Germany, Canada, and the United States produce a steady stream of articles and books on the Chinese Catholic Church.[20] Many of these publications focus on disputes among bishops and priests over the legitimacy of the "open" Church and the "underground" Church. Some of this information is highly partisan, but other information, like that produced by the Holy Spirit Study Centre in Hong Kong, makes a serious effort to strike a balance.

Partisan or not, a common limitation on most of the documentation produced by Catholic study centers is that it does not give a clear picture of life at the grass roots. There are books about the lives of ordinary Catholics, but often they are so concerned with being uplifting that they leave out the gritty details of life.[21] Still, some of them provide useful information on how Catholics live and what they have suffered. My principle for interpreting them was to bracket the inspirational piety and to use only those parts that accorded with the blurred mix of idealism and ordinary human failings that I had discerned in my ethnography.

From the People's Republic of China come *Tianfeng* (Heaven's wind) and other official Church publications written under the supervision of the Chinese Catholic Patriotic Association. Sometimes these provide useful details, but they do not say anything that the government would not approve. Several academic journals, notably *Zongjiao* (Religion) and *Dangdai Zongjiao Yanjiou* (Research on contemporary religion), provide some theoretical analysis, survey research, and ethnographic data.[22]

One extremely useful text from China, however, is a mimeographed collection of articles written for internal circulation in 1987 by a team of investigators from the philosophy department at Beijing University; these articles describe the research they conducted in Shanxi Province. The research, they say, was carried out with the aid of local Catholics and with the government Religious Affairs Bureau. The articles are written from the point of view of people who see religion as a problem, not a blessing, for China. But they are extremely detailed, and they note many positive aspects of Catholic communities and also criticize the ways the government was carrying out its policy toward religion. Their descriptions of the daily practices of rural Catholics accord well with the ethnographic information gathered by Fan Lizhu and myself, and I have relied heavily on these articles to supplement my ethnography.

One final methodological issue is raised by the northern bias of my research locale. If I had done my fieldwork in, say, Guangdong Province, I would have probably developed a more optimistic view than I have of the Church.[23] Indeed, if one studies almost any aspect of Chinese social life from the vantage point of Guangdong, one comes away with a more optimistic picture than if one studies northern China because the south—especially the southern coastal areas—is more prosperous, has a greater variety of ties to the outside world, and is less constrained by rigid political control from the Party center in Beijing. Because of these factors in Guangdong, there is less conflict with the government and much less conflict between the underground Church and the official Church than in the parts of Hebei Province that I studied most closely.

How representative, then, are my findings for China as a whole? Mainly through Hong Kong, I did gather information that enabled me to show what difference the relative openness in provinces like Guangdong sometimes makes in the life of the Catholic Church. (But not always. There have been some severe conflicts between the Church and the government in Shanghai and in Zhejiang Province, coastal areas that are almost as prosperous and open to outside influence as Guang-

Map 2. Hebei Province and its environs, with Catholic sites discussed in this book.

dong, although Catholics there belong largely to marginalized groups, like fisher folk,[24] who have not benefited proportionally from the rising prosperity.)[25] But since the more vivid details of the ethnography are from the north, readers may be overly impressed with the problems of the Church in that context. Underlying these issues of geographical bias is a larger—and for now unanswerable—question about the future development of China: will the more open, free, pluralistic southern coastal regions bring change to the north and to the interior regions; or will the north stifle the south; or, in the mid-term future, will China become increasingly decentralized, with different regions developing distinctive political economies (the most likely possibility, in my view)? Although I will not be able to resolve these issues in this book, I will at least regularly show how they bear on my interpretations.

CIVIL SOCIETY AND THE CATHOLIC CHURCH

Most of the chapters that follow describe an uncivil Chinese Catholic Church, especially in the densely Catholic regions of Hebei, Henan, Shandong, and Shanxi. As we shall see in Chapter 1, Chinese Catholics, in common with most of the people in the rural hinterlands where the Church is at its strongest, are focused on vertical relationships of authority and dependence more than on wide horizontal relationships of reciprocity and cooperation. At the same time, because of the political circumstances facing the Chinese Catholic Church, the Church has no unambiguous way to get the kind of hierarchical leadership it thinks it needs. This difficulty leads to a bitter, indeed, tragic factionalism within the Church.

As we shall see in Chapter 2, although Catholics exhibit a great deal of solidarity at the village level, it is often a narrowly focused, belligerent solidarity that makes them hostile to outsiders. As Chapter 3 shows, Catholics are often more concerned about their personal salvation than alive to the interests of others, especially non-Catholics, and, rather than expanding their loyalties and interests, they aspire to live in self-contained communities—a "world of God," as some Catholics interviewed for this book put it—in which religious life is closely intertwined with local economic and political life.

Moreover, in the course of this exposition, we will notice that the Chinese Catholic Church shares these uncivil qualities with many other communities that are filling the social space opened up by the Chinese government's inability to extend its control throughout society. Does this mean, then, that China will not develop a civil society or, if it does, that the Catholic Church will not play a positive part in this development? Not necessarily. As we shall see in Chapter 4, many of these uncivil qualities are the result of the Church's successful adaptation to the premodern institutions of Chinese rural life. In the cities, a different kind of Catholicism is tentatively emerging, which may have more potential for civility. Finally, in Chapter 5, I argue that the lack of civility manifested in the Chinese Catholic Church, and in many other Chinese associations, is the result of a particular social context: an agrarian society in which economic, political, and social relationships often remain intricately intertwined at the local level; a history of harsh repression; and an authoritarian, hierarchical culture. If we see how this configuration of social institutions, these historical memories, and these cultural resources have combined to develop the uncivil characteristics of the Chinese Catholic Church, we can see how these characteristics might be changing. In some parts of the world, including Hong Kong and Taiwan, the Catholic Church is in fact a vital participant in civil society. With the right leadership in a changing Chinese social context, it could play such a role in mainland China.

CHAPTER ONE

Hierarchy and History

*The Problem of Authority in the
Chinese Catholic Church*

Sitting in his one-hundred-square-foot apartment off a narrow Tianjin alley, seventy-year-old Mr. Wang testified to his humble faith. The darkness was fitfully dispelled by a flickering fluorescent tube; the walls were adorned with pictures of Jesus, Mary, and Joseph, all portrayed, in the saccharine kitsch of Western folk piety, with flowing brown hair and soft, feminine features. Mr. Wang came from a village in Xian County in Hebei Province, where everybody has the same surname, everybody knows everybody else, everybody claims the same common ancestor, and everybody is Catholic.

"I don't know much about Catholic doctrine," he admitted. He did not have a lot of "theoretical ability." But "I have my own opinions, and what I believe is what my parents believed." He arose every morning around 4:00 A.M., did his exercises, and walked to the 5:00 A.M. Mass. He told us how his faith gave him the strength to nurse his wife during the ten years that she was bedridden from diabetes. In his slow, deliberate voice, he recalled their last hours together. "In the morning and the evening, we would say the rosary together. That is our Catholic custom. That day, I got up earlier than her and said my morning prayers. Then we started praying together. Twenty minutes later, she collapsed. I couldn't revive her. I rushed to get my kids and the priest. But it was too late. That day was a feast day of the Virgin Mary. So my old lady is together with Mary. The priest comforted me. Of course I felt very sad. But I also felt comforted. It *very* rarely happens that people die right when they're saying their prayers. When I thought about this, I felt very happy. She's with the Lord."

He didn't usually "open books"; indeed, he might be considered only semiliterate. But in the middle of our conversation, he said he had something to show us, and from a cabinet drawer he carefully pulled an old notebook. Inside he had laboriously copied contents of a long chart that hung on a wall of the church rectory. It depicted the history of the world, the history of the Catholic Church, and the history of China. It began at the top with God's creation of Adam and Eve. Then it split into two columns. One column depicted the Biblical story of "salvation history": from the Tower of Babel and Noah's ark (there were little pictures of these, which Mr. Wang had carefully copied) to Abraham and Moses down to Jesus and onward through the history of the Catholic Church. The other column was the history of China: from the sage emperors down to the Republic of China in the twentieth century (the chart was published in 1939). Toward the bottom of the chart, the histories came together as the Catholic Church was established in China.

Though the old man did not usually read books, he had a profound sense of history. He talked about the Kangxi emperor's edict of toleration for Christianity (in 1692).[1] "Kangxi was never baptized. But he had a lot of understanding of Catholicism." His belief, Mr. Wang said, was a foundation for his life. As he told the Catholic story, it connected him through his parents and ancestors to a story that included great emperors like Kangxi and famous missionaries like Matteo Ricci and went all the way back through Jesus to the sage emperors and finally to Adam and Eve.

Mr. Wang's sense of history is not idiosyncratic. I saw the same chart that he had so lovingly copied hanging in remote village churches as well as in Mr. Wang's church in Tianjin. Many other Catholics spoke of the heritage of their faith not just as an abstract legacy of ideas but as a concrete connection in blood, through their ancestors to the beginnings of history. This vision of identity is hierarchical as well as historical. Traditions of ancestor worship give ordinary Chinese, especially peasants, a strong sense of continuity with preceding generations. Chinese Catholicism builds on this vision. It tells its followers that they are connected not only with their blood ancestors but with a lineage of great people. The chart that Mr. Wang had copied was like an elite ancestor chart, full of emperors and popes and great saints. It said in effect to Mr. Wang that these great people too were part of his lineage. He and his ancestors belong with them, even though they occupy a lower place.[2]

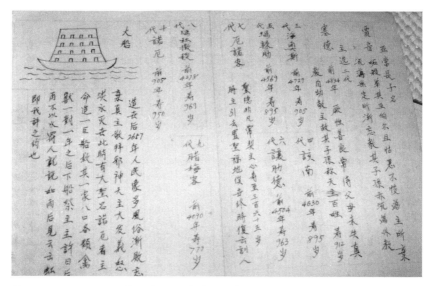

Figure 4. Mr. Wang's hand-copied chart of "salvation history." Photograph by Richard Madsen.

The grand ceremonies of Catholic worship cement this sense of being glorified through a hierarchical connection. Most of the faithful are of humble origin. In the nineteenth and twentieth centuries, missionaries had relatively little success with urban, educated elites. The great majority of Catholics are in the countryside; or if they now live in the city, they are, like Mr. Wang, but a generation removed from rural roots. But their churches are soaring edifices. Cathedrals like St. Joseph's in Tianjin are imposing, neo-Gothic or neo-Romanesque buildings. Filled with pomp, the sacred rituals lift ordinary people out of humdrum lives into a magnificent world.

It is not simply a heavenly world, but a world constituted through the earthly splendor of the hierarchical Church. Churches and chapels in rural villages are miniature copies of the big cathedrals. Local liturgies are reflections, albeit pale ones, of the great rituals in the diocesan centers. And the diocesan cathedrals and episcopal ceremonies are reflections of the glories of St. Peter's Basilica in the Holy See of Rome. Standing at the apex of the Catholic hierarchy, the pope takes on a legendary stature. A local Catholic village leader told us how he had heard that when China's first cardinal, Cardinal Tian, visited the Vatican in the late 1940s, he was met at the plane by two angels in radiant robes who led him to his audience with the pope.

Modern European Catholics have mostly lost this vision of themselves as part of a heavenly world reflected through the earthly splendor of an ecclesiastical hierarchy. In such places, Catholicism has become a middle-class religion, a faith of people who mostly take pride in being able to take care of themselves, who are a little embarrassed usually at basking in the glory of earthly hierarchies. When they do participate in the full pomp and circumstance of the hierarchical Church on special occasions, like a papal visit, they do so as tourists visiting an exotic destination—the visit may be thrilling, but one does not feel at home there. Influenced no doubt by this modern middle-class sensibility, the documents of the second Vatican Council picture the Church as a community, a "people of God," rather than as a hierarchy, and they envision the pope not as an absolute monarch but as the head of a "college" of bishops, to whose collective wisdom he is morally obliged to listen.[3]

But the Chinese Catholic Church still adheres largely to an older hierarchical vision. Having until recently been cut off from communication with the outside world, it has not learned the lessons of Vatican II, and, in addition, the hierarchical vision is deeply congenial to its believers' experience and cultural traditions. If one's life is poor and drab, it means a great deal to feel that one is a vital participant in a majestic cosmos. Moreover, the Catholic idea that the individual gains meaning through participation in a centralized hierarchical order resonates with a Confucian tradition that still exerts a strong, if subtle, influence on Chinese life. It resonates also with a vision of China's greatness that is projected by the Communists. For all their egalitarian ideology, they have in practice envisioned China as a vast hierarchical polity subordinated to an all-powerful center. So when Chinese Catholics participate in their Church's displays of hierarchical order, they feel not like tourists but like pilgrims who are finally seeing a glimpse of their true and final home.

Whereas in modern Western Catholicism the Church as community is often seen in some sense as being in tension with the Church as hierarchy, in China hierarchy and community are much more closely connected and mutually reinforcing. Catholics have a strong sense of community precisely because they can see their small community as connected hierarchically to a larger earthly community, which is itself a representation of divine community. This hierarchical imagination was a pillar of strength in hard times, like the Maoist era, when the Church was under implacable persecution and Catholics faced stark choices. But in soft times, like the present, when the persecution has lessened, the issues are less stark, and the choices are more ambiguous, the hierarchical imagination becomes a dangerous liability, a foundation of sand.

CATHOLIC HIERARCHY AND
CHINESE POLITICAL HIERARCHY

One of the strengths of the Church's hierarchical identity has been its resonance with Chinese culture. The traditional Catholic sense that local community life was made meaningful through its connection with a hierarchical order of cosmic proportions is similar to the ideology of state Confucianism in the Ming and Qing dynasties. Precisely because the Church's conception of hierarchy seemed so "Chinese," the missionaries who implanted the Church in China in the late sixteenth century sometimes identified so fully with the Chinese imperial state that their own Catholic identity became confused. The resultant internal ecclesiastical controversies led to a backlash in the Church against Chinese hierarchies and sometimes to fatal conflict with powerful, indigenous Chinese authorities. Soft times then gave way to hard times, and the Church's strong hierarchical discipline enabled it to withstand persecution.

Although there had been two earlier waves of missionary activity, the first in the seventh century, when Nestorian Christians came to the western frontier of the Chinese empire, and the second in the thirteenth century, when Franciscans came to Yuan China, the sixteenth-century wave has lasted to the present. Jesuits, Franciscans, Dominicans, and confreres of the Société des Missions Etrangères de Paris (MEP) represented a Counter Reformation missionary movement that took advantage of new routes opened by the Age of Exploration to win converts to make up for the losses suffered in the Reformation. In reaction to the Reformation, they brought to China a faith that emphasized even more than medieval Christianity the hierarchical structure of the Church.

The Jesuits, led by Matteo Ricci, aimed to gain influence with the political and intellectual elites of the Ming dynasty. To do so, they accommodated their message to the ideology of state Confucianism. In effect, they said that Catholicism was consistent with those ritual practices that linked family hierarchy to the hierarchical order centered in the emperor, the Son of Heaven. In this approach, Catholic hierarchy could be seen as intertwined with and as reinforcing the imperial hierarchy. The Qing emperors, who took over from the Ming after 1644, legitimized their reign by claiming that it too was based on state Confucianism.

The Jesuits continued their same approach with the Qing elites, and they eventually gained access to the highest echelons of the Qing court. One of the Jesuits, Ferdinand Verbiest, became a personal friend and advisor to the Kangxi emperor. Although the emperor did not convert to Catholicism, he issued an edict of toleration in 1692, which asserted that Christianity was consistent with Confucian orthodoxy. Even today, old Mr. Wang knows about Kangxi's edict of toleration, and he sees this edict as a proof that Catholicism can connect his humble life with the grand hierarchies not only of the universal Church but of the best in the Chinese political tradition.

At the same time that the Jesuits were preaching their gospel of accommodation in the late Ming and early Qing, however, Catholic rivals to the Jesuits were arguing that such accommodation was wrong. The Jesuits contended that the rituals used by the Chinese to bury their dead and to honor Confucius were just a way of practicing the basic Christian virtues of honoring parents and respecting legitimate authority. The Dominicans, Franciscans, and MEP members who were the Jesuits' rivals argued that such rituals amounted to the worship of false gods. Under this interpretation, Chinese Catholics should indeed practice all the social virtues that their non-Catholic neighbors considered the mark of a good person. They should honor their parents, pray for their dead, venerate their ancestors, and even respect the political rule of the emperor as much as non-Christians. But they could not celebrate these virtues through those indigenous rituals that connected family life with a sacred cosmic order mediated by the emperor. They could celebrate them only through those ritual forms used in European Catholicism.[4]

The Chinese emperor was not only a political ruler but a ritual leader. His main role was to carry out rituals that would mediate between Heaven (which, Jesuit rationalizations to the contrary, was envisioned as a personal deity) and earth and thus ensure a well-ordered, peaceful, and prosperous world. His political power was dependent on his ability to properly carry out and safeguard the rituals of state Confucianism. From the point of view of Chinese emperors, then, Catholics who rejected these basic rituals were participating in a hierarchical cosmos that rivaled rather than complemented that ritually presided over by the emperor. Even if Catholics still submitted to political authorities, their disavowal of Confucian rituals would ultimately undermine imperial Chinese authority.

The Rites Controversy lasted most of a century. In the end, the Jesuits lost. In 1704, Pope Clement XI issued an edict condemning the

Chinese rites, a condemnation confirmed and made even more rigid by Pope Benedict XIV in 1742. As a result, the Vatican ended the Jesuit mission to China, and the Kangxi emperor and his successors declared Catholicism a heterodox sect, proscribing foreign missionary activity.[5]

In the nineteenth century, as the power of the Qing dynasty waned, foreign missionary activity resumed again, this time Protestant as well as Catholic. This wave was made possible because of Western imperialism. The unequal treaties signed after the notorious Opium Wars gave missionaries the right to travel throughout China, to own property (and to recover property confiscated by emperors after the Rites Controversy), to build churches, and in general to carry out missionary activity however they pleased.

By papal decree, Catholic missionaries had to take an oath not to accommodate any traditional Chinese rituals. This prohibition effectively precluded any conversion of elites, whether local gentry or imperial officials. The Catholic Church did prove attractive to some ordinary peasants, however. For them, the Church offered a hierarchical alternative to the imperial system. Catholic missionaries made the trappings of local officials their own. For instance, by the end of the nineteenth century, Catholic bishops used the insignia of a provincial governor and were carried around in sedan chairs in the manner of someone of that rank. Missionaries could adopt these trappings because they were backed by the power of their home governments (and, no matter what country they came from, by the power of the French, who assumed a "right of protectorate" over the Church in China).

If the ritual hierarchy expressed in state Confucianism was deeply intertwined with the political structure of the imperial Chinese state, the ritual hierarchy expressed in nineteenth-century Catholicism in China became just as deeply intertwined with the political structure of Western imperialism. To be a Catholic was to enjoy a special relationship not only with God or with the pope but also with the foreign powers that were attempting to dominate China. If one were a Catholic, one could benefit from foreign-subsidized church buildings, schools, and clinics, and, in time of need, one might receive foreign-subsidized food. Because missionaries were protected by the right of "extraterritoriality" and because, according to the unequal treaties, this right was extended to those under their tutelage, their converts could also enjoy the political benefits of immunity from Chinese law.[6]

Chinese Catholics, then, belonged to a different world than other Chinese. Though they shared the same ethical values and indeed shared with most other Chinese a sense of the importance of hierarchy, they participated both ritually and politically in a different hierarchical order. To maintain this alternative order, missionaries created Catholic enclaves. Their assumption was that one could not be a Catholic merely by holding the faith within one's heart. One had to be a member of a community dominated by the Church hierarchy. Missionaries were instructed to refuse baptism to individuals who did not belong to a Catholic community—to a village or a neighborhood where most of the residents were Catholic. Missionaries tried to make these communities like little Christendoms, where socially, economically, and politically life was closely intertwined with the Church.

By the late nineteenth century, the privileges enjoyed by Catholics and their aloofness from the ordinary social life of their neighbors gained them enmity. In 1899–1900, they became one of the main targets of the Boxer rebellion, a rural movement led by martial-arts experts and directed against foreign influence.[7] The Boxers laid siege to churches and killed several hundred missionaries and thousands of their converts. While the Communist government now celebrates the Boxer rebellion as an uprising of the popular masses against imperial rule, Catholics recount a different history in their villages. Especially northern Chinese Catholics of Mr. Wang's generation tell stories passed on to them by their parents: how the Boxers surrounded their villages while the Catholics retreated behind the walls of the church and how the Catholics heroically fought off the Boxers until the Virgin Mary, Our Lady Queen of Victories, herself appeared (some people say she was joined by Jesus and Joseph) and drove them away. Passed down through oral tradition, the Catholic stories of the suffering endured at the hands of the Boxers and the triumph achieved with the help of Holy Mary powerfully reaffirm a distinctive Catholic identity and destiny.

The Catholics we interviewed around Tianjin and in Hebei also told stories of how the faith had flourished after the suppression of the Boxers by the "Eight Nation Allied Army" in 1900. The Europeans forced the Qing court to pay large indemnities and to make restitution to those who had been harmed by the Boxers. Churches that had been destroyed were now rebuilt, and a large amount of resources flowed into Catholic communities. The fastest growth in the Catholic Church took place in the first decade of the twentieth century, the decade after the Boxer uprising.

After the collapse of the Qing dynasty in 1911, Catholic missionaries abandoned the most flagrant affectations of imperial privilege. Bishops did not claim the status of provincial governors. Foreign military power was not so frequently used to enforce the privileges of Chinese Catholics. But the religious hierarchy of the Church remained intertwined with worldly structures of power and status. Foreign missionaries were reluctant to give up their control over the Chinese Church. Although in the 1910s a few courageous Church reformers like the Belgian missionary Vincent Lebbe advocated the ordination of more Chinese priests and the preparation of some of these priests to become bishops in charge of the Church, most foreign missionaries resisted. Partly in an effort to break the dominance of French missionaries over the Church, the Vatican moved toward the creation of native clergy. In his 1919 encyclical *Maximum Illud,* Pope Benedict XV warned that "it would be regrettable, indeed, were any of the missionaries to be so forgetful of their dignity as to think more of their earthly than of their heavenly country, and were too bent on extending its earthly glory and power." In 1926, Pope Pius XI personally ordained the first group of six Chinese bishops.[8]

Foreign missionaries continued, however, to dominate the Chinese Church. Claiming that it was not yet mature, they in many instances resisted the ordination of Chinese bishops and kept most of the Chinese bishops they did ordain in subordinate positions within the Church hierarchy. For its part, the Vatican continued to treat the Chinese Catholic Church as a mission territory rather than as a national Church. Thus, the affairs of the Church were controlled from Rome by the Vatican Office of the Propagation of the Faith (Propaganda Fidei) rather than by a Chinese national council of bishops.

In theory, the hierarchical order represented in the ritual life and theological imagination of the Catholic Church is not the same thing as an administrative chain of command. But in the nineteenth and early twentieth centuries, ritual hierarchy was closely identified with administrative hierarchy. To be a Catholic was to be under the centralized administrative control of the Vatican; and in China it was also to be under the control mostly of foreign priests backed by foreign political powers.

Only in 1946, after the Sino-Japanese war, did the Vatican remove the Chinese Church from the jurisdiction of Propaganda Fidei and give it the status of a national Church, under the formal jurisdiction of a native hierarchy. At this time, the pope named the bishop of Beijing, Thomas Tian Gengxin, to be the first Chinese cardinal. Nonetheless, less than 20 percent of the dioceses/prefectures in China were led by Chinese bishops.[9]

THE CATHOLIC CHURCH
AND THE COMMUNIST PARTY

By this time, civil war was breaking out in China, and the days of foreign domination over the Chinese Church were numbered. Once they
took power, the Communists quickly expelled all foreign missionaries,
Protestant as well as Catholic, and strove to exert control over all religious life. The clash with the Catholic Church was especially bitter because of the hierarchical nature of the Church.

The Communist regime mirrored the Catholic Church in its obses-
sion with hierarchy. All power radiated from the Party center in Beijing,
the atmosphere of which, with its obsessive status consciousness and its
constant intrigues, was similar to that of the old imperial court. Radiated
through layers and layers of bureaucracy, this central authority created
subordinate microcosms of itself at different levels. From the most remote villages on up, a ladder of Party committees was intertwined with
state institutions. Like the relation of Catholic parish to diocese to national bishops' conference to Holy See, the lower levels were supposed
to perform the same functions as the higher, but they derived their legitimacy from their subordination to the higher. Also like the Catholic
Church, the Chinese Communist state, especially under Mao Zedong,
claimed to be not just an instrument of power but a representation of
the moral order linking individuals to China's destiny and indeed to the
ultimate purposes of history.[10]

Precisely because it claimed for itself a quasi-religious status, the
Maoist regime could not tolerate an independent Chinese Catholic
Church. An independent Catholic Church posed not just practical political problems arising from its capacity to harbor political dissidents
but a fundamental symbolic challenge to the regime. By its independent
existence, the Catholic Church challenged the quasi-religious claims
made by the Maoist state. The Chinese government could tolerate the
Church only if the Church were subordinated to the government's own
hierarchy.

The leaders of the Church could not accept such subordination.
They called on the Catholic faithful to endure persecution rather than
compromise their faith under the new regime. Given the kinds of religious claims made by the Catholic Church, there was probably nothing
else that responsible Church leaders could do. But the Catholic Church
helped make a difficult situation even worse because of the quasi-
political ambitions of some of its leaders. Since the 1930s, Archbishop

Yu Bin of Nanjing (he later became a cardinal and was made president of the Catholic Fu Jen University in Taipei) was a major international advocate of Chiang Kai-shek and the Nationalist Party.[11] If the Maoist government was a political hierarchy with quasi-religious pretensions, the Catholic Church was a religious hierarchy with quasi-political pretensions. And, each in its own way, the Chinese government and the Catholic Church became plagued by arrogant, insensitive bureaucracies.

Particularly troublesome was the way in which foreign Church bureaucrats, with little understanding of Chinese society, demanded that the Church take a maximally provocative, aggressive stance against the Communist regime. In 1946, just after the formal establishment of a native Church hierarchy, the Vatican posted Archbishop Antonio Riberi to China as its first internuncio (an ambassador charged both with representing the interests of the Vatican to the government and with ensuring that the internal policies of the Church conform with Vatican policy). Riberi openly supported the Nationalist government and urged Catholics to follow that government's anti-Communist policy as a matter of Catholic faith. In 1947, following instructions from Rome, he forbade Chinese Catholics from joining any Communist-controlled or influenced organization. In 1948, he organized the Legion of Mary, an elite organization of Catholic activists, whom he charged with fighting communism.[12]

On the eve of the Communist victory, Riberi and his Vatican superiors issued even more stringent demands. Kim-kwong Chan recounts:

> In July, 1949, three months before the formation of the [People's Republic of China], Rome issued an order to all Catholics to oppose and to boycott any communist influence. Riberi passed this order on to the [bishops] in China. . . . This order forbade any Catholic to join or to sympathize with [the Chinese Communist Party], to publish, to read, to write, or to propagate any communist literature; violation of this order would lead to the termination of receiving the Sacraments and even excommunication. . . . In July 28, 1951, Riberi conveyed the order from Rome which extended the ecclesial punishment even to the parents or guardians of those who had violated the decree issued [in] July 1949; this new order also broadened the scope for excommunication.[13]

Meanwhile, Riberi's headquarters in Shanghai "published many booklets to strengthen the faith of the Catholics, to encourage them in following the teaching of the Church, to attack the communist ideology, and to equip them in the fight against the communists."[14]

The Vatican's aggressive and uncompromising anti-Communist

stance, enforced through Archbishop Riberi, put an enormous burden on Chinese Catholics, especially the Chinese clergy. The Church was a tiny and vulnerable part of Chinese society. An explicit proclamation of anti-Communism was an invitation to martyrdom. Foreigners like Riberi who imposed the anti-Communist stance faced severe harassment and expulsion,[15] but many of the Chinese they left behind faced long imprisonment, torture, and sometimes death. In many Eastern European countries, the Church, though clearly in principle anti-Communist, took a less confrontational stance and achieved tense but workable accommodations with Communist regimes. With regard to China, however, Vatican officials seemed more rigidly concerned with the purity of their principles than with the fate of the Catholics under their care.

In line with its policy toward other organized religions, the Chinese Communist Party established a "mass organization" to oversee the activities of the Church. Supposedly representing groups within society rather than government, a mass organization was in fact established by the government, was supervised by the Party, and was supposed to be a "transmission belt" for government policies rather than a way for citizens to defend their political interests. Under the political system established by the Party, no social activity could take place outside such organizations.[16] In most cases the activities of mass organizations were monitored and controlled by Party members chosen from within the organization. But members of religious groups could not (officially) be Party members (some reportedly were members in secret) because their beliefs contradicted the atheism required of Party members. These groups were placed in mass organizations under the government's Religious Affairs Bureau and supervised by the Party's United Front Work Department. Leaders within these religious mass organizations were carefully selected by government and Party authorities, who chose people willing to cooperate with Party policies.

The mass organization for controlling the Catholic Church was called the Chinese Catholic Patriotic Association. As early as the autumn of 1950, the Chinese government began to lay the foundations for this organization by establishing local "Catholic reform committees." In the name of anti-imperialism, these committees were supposed to help the Church implement the "three autonomies": Church governance, finance, and propagation were supposed to be independent of all foreign agencies and under Chinese control, which in practice meant Chinese government control. Riberi denounced this movement, and the Vatican issued a decree excommunicating all those who participated. A year later, Riberi was expelled from China, followed within the next two years by almost all the remaining Catholic missionaries. In January of 1952, Pope Pius XII issued an encyclical defending the missionaries and condemning Catholic cooperation in the movement for the "three autonomies." [17]

At the same time that it was establishing the "Catholic reform committees" (which were eventually renamed "Patriotic Associations"), the Chinese government was imprisoning clergy and laity whom it considered disloyal. Most active Catholics were inclined to resist. It was clear enough that the autonomy they were supposed to claim from the Vatican would only place them even more under the control of a Chinese government that was hostile to their religion. As Catholic resistance continued, arrests and persecution increased. By the end of 1955, fifteen hundred Shanghai Catholics had been arrested, including Bishop Gong Pinmei, the most influential Catholic leader in China. Similar waves of arrests took place throughout the country.[18]

Those in the most poignant predicament were the clergy. The government put enormous pressure on them to join its compliant Patriotic Associations. The Vatican threatened them with excommunication if they did so but could do nothing to protect them. Trained to believe that loyalty to the Vatican was essential to the Catholic faith, the laity expected their clergy to resist the government and usually shunned those who did give in to government pressure. But the laity could not help their priests and bishops, and as long as they had not been activists in organizations like the Legion of Mary and did not express active support of their priests, the laity could stay out of trouble. Nuns, priests, and bishops were left terribly alone.

Most of them resisted the government and suffered some form of imprisonment. What sustained them was a spirit of martyrdom, a belief that their suffering would win them a place in heaven combined with a sense that their fellow Catholics, however furtively, greatly honored them for their sacrifice. A minority broke under the pressure and joined the Patriotic Associations. Others, including several bishops, joined the Patriotic Associations out of some combination of opportunism, resentment at the patronizing treatment they had received from foreign missionaries and the Vatican, and a sense of responsibility for keeping the Church publicly alive under difficult circumstances.

In 1957, the government established the national Chinese Catholic Patriotic Association, centralizing control over local Patriotic Associations. The leaders of this association denounced the Vatican and, with

the encouragement of the Communist Party, began electing and conse-
crating bishops without the approval of Rome. Pope Pius XII responded
with condemnation. By 1962, about forty-two bishops had been chosen
and consecrated by bishops connected with the Chinese Catholic Patriotic Association.[19] From the point of view of the Vatican, these conse-
crations were "illicit" but "valid," a subtle theological distinction. Since
the consecration rituals were carried out in the proper manner, the bishops were truly bishops—when they administered the sacraments, the
sacraments truly conveyed God's grace. But since Rome had not approved their consecration, these bishops and their followers were acting
disobediently.[20] In an emergency—for instance, if a person were on the
verge of death—a good Catholic might receive the sacraments from one
of these bishops or from a priest ordained by them. Under normal circumstances, however, a good Catholic should not attend a Mass or go
to a confession conducted by one of these illicit bishops or anyone associated with them, have a marriage blessed by them, or receive any of
the other sacraments from them. Catholics who did would commit a
mortal sin, and if they did not repent, they would go to hell. Whatever
the mix of motives that led some priests and bishops to participate in
the Chinese Catholic Patriotic Association, most ordinary Catholics
seem to have shunned these collaborators. An underground Church
grew up, consisting of congregations who risked punishment by meeting secretly with priests who had refused to cooperate with the Patriotic
Association.

Though it invited persecution, the hierarchical structure of the
Church provided strength. A commitment to that structure kept Chinese Catholics, though scattered throughout the country, unified in
spite of government attempts to drive them apart. From the Catholic
point of view, the Maoist government's quasi-religious claims were so
patently false that most Catholics were united in at least passive opposition to the government's ideology. They also remained clear about who
their real leaders were—those courageous bishops, priests, and nuns
who in their loyalty to the pope suffered prison rather than give in to
government attempts to co-opt the Church through the Chinese Catholic Patriotic Association. Because the government's persecution was
directed mainly against the Church's hierarchical leaders rather than
against its laity, the laity could find quiet inspiration in those martyred
leaders without necessarily having to suffer too much themselves.

The Maoist antireligious policy thus strengthened the solidarity of
Catholic communities. Although the Chinese Catholic Church had no

way of knowing of the reforms initiated by the second Vatican Council in 1964, their experience under persecution constituted in practice one of the lessons that Vatican II taught in theory—that ordinary laypeople have an enormous responsibility for maintaining the vitality of Catholic community. In the absence of priests, Catholic villages and neighborhoods quietly organized themselves to carry out their own devotions. Mothers and grandmothers taught children the basic prayers and doctrines. Lay leaders furtively gave fellow Catholics counsel and guidance.[21]

A strong community spirit helped Catholics survive the persecution of the Cultural Revolution, when all churches were closed or destroyed and all overt religious practice was punished. Few foreign observers expected any more than a tiny Catholic remnant to survive, and they were amazed after the persecution to find the Chinese Catholic community undiminished in size. There were about three million Catholics before 1949. When the persecution lifted after the death of Mao and the overthrow of his supporters, it became apparent that there were about ten million Catholics; the Catholic population had expanded at about the same rate as the Chinese population as a whole.

REFORM, OPENING, AND DIVISION

But the strengths that had allowed the Church to retain its numbers during hard times turned into weaknesses when conditions improved. One improvement was that the Chinese state could no longer make any quasi-religious claims that could rival those of the Catholic Church. The Cultural Revolution destroyed the religious aura that Mao had created around the Communist movement. The Deng Xiaoping regime justified itself through a more pragmatic ideology—"seek the truth from facts." The Chinese state promised no longer to lead the nation to a socialist utopia but only to foster through economic reform the kind of stable economic growth that would allow each individual to improve his or her material well-being. Even as the state withdrew from its religious pretensions, though, the senseless violence of the Cultural Revolution had left the Chinese people with more profound questions than ever before about the ultimate meaning of life. In this moral vacuum, many Chinese were predisposed to look to traditional religion to make sense of the tragedies of history and to sustain new hope for the future.

The policies of "reform and opening" launched by the Deng Xiaoping regime in December 1978 included a relaxation of restrictions on

religious practice and opportunities for religious believers to renew contact with foreign members of their faith. The regime relaxed its restrictions not because of any fondness for religion but out of a recognition
that it was impossible to retain ironclad control over religious practice
while pursuing economic reform. The basic strategy, which was formal-
ized in a 1982 Communist Party directive called "Document 19," seems
to have been one of co-optation.[22] Document 19 recognizes that attempting to eradicate religion completely will only drive it underground. It
advocates permitting religion to flourish within carefully controlled conditions, where it can be monitored and made to serve the state.

Thus, as the new religious policy began to be implemented in 1979,
priests were released from prison; some churches, like the cathedral in
Tianjin, were reopened or rebuilt; some Church property was returned;
convents and seminaries were gradually reestablished. At the same
time, the Chinese Catholic Patriotic Association was revived (after having been shut down during the Cultural Revolution), and the government issued strict regulations restricting Catholic religious practice to
churches registered with the association.

In order to make it acceptable for Catholics to participate in churches
registered with the Chinese Catholic Patriotic Association, the government relaxed its heavy-handed control over the strictly religious aspects
of life.[23] It allowed some priests to practice their ministry without
joining the Association, as long as they did not openly oppose it. (Most
ordinary Catholic laypersons, even if they worship in government-
approved churches, do not belong to the Patriotic Association.) The
government facilitated the establishment of a national conference of
bishops, which was formally separate from the politically oriented Chinese Catholic Patriotic Association and was given latitude to make
decisions on theological, pastoral, and liturgical matters. The national
conference of bishops was even allowed to say that it recognized the
spiritual primacy of the pope and to reinstate the prayers in the Mass
that are ordinarily said for the pope, prayers that had previously been
deleted by order of the Chinese Catholic Patriotic Association. In the
early 1980s, the government even took some tentative steps to reach a
rapprochement with the Vatican.[24]

This should have been a happy time for the Chinese Catholic Church,
a second spring of religious life. But it was a stormy spring, marked by
tragic conflict not just between Catholics and the government but
among Catholics themselves. The problem was that the Catholic need

for an unambiguous hierarchical leadership could no longer be fulfilled. Many claimants for leadership positions came forward, but no central authority could effectively adjudicate among rival claims.

One set of claims came from the public Church, the Catholic community that was able to function openly as long as it abided by the regulations of the Religious Affairs Bureau and the Chinese Catholic Patriotic Association.[25] As the Chinese government lost its religious aura, some Catholics thought they might cooperate with it on a purely pragmatic basis. The government now allowed priests and even bishops who had never cooperated with the Chinese Catholic Patriotic Association—clergy members who had indeed sometimes spent years in prison because of their loyalty to Vatican directives—to resume their ministry as long as they did not violate government regulations. However, these priests would have to work within a religious context that was still formally controlled at the top by the Chinese Catholic Patriotic Association, which was led by some Catholics who were widely despised as collaborators.

Could Catholic clergy legitimately work under these circumstances? Years of struggling in isolation had given many Catholics the habit of looking into their hearts or of looking to their peers for answers to such a question. At the same time, they felt compelled by doctrine and by tradition to look to the Vatican. Yet the Vatican's directives were ambiguous. Some parts of the Vatican, especially the Secretariat of State, seemed to be groping for a rapprochement with the Chinese government. In 1993, for instance, one of the Vatican's top diplomats, Cardinal Roger Etchegary, came to Beijing as an "unofficial" guest at the opening of the Asian Games, and it was widely assumed that he engaged in quiet negotiations with the Chinese government. Such gestures seemed to give credence to those Chinese Catholics willing to make some compromises with the government for the sake of gaining the ability to practice their faith openly. Some prominent Asian cardinals and archbishops, like the Cardinal Archbishop of Manila and the Archbishop of Tokyo, visited China and said Mass in the open churches approved by the Chinese Catholic Patriotic Association. In some places, secret emissaries from the Vatican visited Chinese Church leaders, often under the guise of tourists, and recited memorized directives in Latin conveying official Vatican approval for certain bishops to be leaders of their dioceses even though their appointments had also been approved by the Chinese Catholic Patriotic Association.[26] Published reports in the West state that as many as one-third of the bishops of the open Church have received such Vatican approval, and reliable unpublished reports put the number considerably higher.[27]

At the same time, other parts of the Vatican, especially Propaganda Fidei, were issuing directives encouraging the rise of an underground Church. In Eastern Europe, in the late 1970s, the Vatican had encouraged the development of underground churches by relaxing provisions of canon law requiring a formal course of study for candidates for the priesthood and formal Vatican control over the appointment of new bishops. This relaxation allowed underground bishops to appoint successors and to ordain new priests without having to maintain risky communications with Rome. In 1978, some aging underground bishops in China asked the Vatican for similar modifications of canon law. Propaganda Fidei issued a secret document, "Faculties and Privileges Granted to Clergy and Laymen Who Reside in China under Difficult Circumstances," which gave underground clergy great flexibility in managing their own affairs.[28] With the ascension of the assertive new Polish pope John Paul II in 1979, the Vatican seemed even firmer in its resolve to help the underground Church.

Out of touch with the Vatican on a regular basis, the underground bishops then took the initiative to ordain a large number of new priests and to consecrate new bishops. The training these "black priests" (as they are called in some places by Catholics and non-Catholics alike) received usually consisted of a direct apprenticeship to another underground priest. Since the choice of new bishops was uncontrolled by the Vatican's bureaucratic procedures, the underground Church began to be pervaded with patron-client relationships.[29]

The underground Church has garnered strong support, both moral and material, from outside China. In early 1988, the Chinese government released from detention one of the most staunch symbols of loyalty to the Vatican, the Archbishop of Shanghai, Gong Pinmei, after a confinement of about thirty-three years, apparently as a gesture of conciliation toward the international human-rights community and perhaps toward the underground Church. The archbishop was then allowed, in effect, to go into exile in the United States, ostensibly for medical reasons. The pope announced in 1991 that Archbishop Gong had been made a cardinal of the Church. The Chinese government and, at the government's bidding, leaders of the Chinese Catholic Patriotic Association were furious that the pope had thus publicly honored someone who had so prominently stood against them. Although Cardinal Gong, now in his nineties, is presently in a nursing home in Connecticut, out of touch with most Church activities, his nephew in the United States has established a foundation to support the cause of the underground Church. This foundation has attracted substantial financial support from Catholics in the United States and around the world. Its activities are complemented by those of several other foundations: the Puebla Institute (connected with Freedom House) and Free the Fathers (connected with right-wing political figures like Robert Dornan and Phyllis Schlafly), which publicize human-rights abuses against leaders of the underground Church and provide financial support. Prominent clergymen from dioceses in the United States and Europe, as well as Asia, secretly send money to underground Catholics. And the Vatican, somewhat like the Chinese Communist Party itself, is a faction-ridden administrative apparatus, as much feudal as bureaucratic, that harbors groups with diverse agendas regarding China. With the hope of normalizing relationships with the People's Republic, some of these groups want to be conciliatory toward the Chinese government, and they are disposed to encourage reconciliation and cooperation with the official Church. Other factions in the Vatican, however, remain resolutely opposed to compromise and are staunchly in support of the underground.

As the open churches were filling with worshipers, the leaders of the underground Church were becoming increasingly defiant. Underground Catholic defiance reached a high plateau in that year of dissent, 1989. But, interestingly, it was almost a half year after the June 4 crackdown that leaders of the underground Church committed their boldest act. In November, at a clandestine meeting in Shanxi Province, a group of underground bishops established an alternative bishops' conference. Informants tipped off the police about this meeting, and many of its leaders were arrested. This crackdown still did not squelch underground Church activity. Emboldened perhaps by the role played by Eastern European churches in the collapse of Communism, the underground Church has become more confrontational than ever. And frightened by the same Eastern European events, the government has become more repressive.[30] The human-rights organization Asia Watch has documented the escalating frequency of the detention and torture of bishops and priests (and also Protestant clergy) by public security officers. Perhaps desperate to find ways to stem the causes of social unrest, some officials have resorted to increasingly brutal forms of intimidation.[31]

In the eyes of many Chinese Catholics, one of the more outrageous acts of brutality took place in April of 1992. Eighty-five-year-old Bishop

Fan Xueyan, of Baoding, Hebei Province, who was perhaps, next to Archbishop Gong Pinmei, the most influential and widely respected of the bishops who had resisted the government's attempts to co-opt and control the Church, died in police custody a day before the end of a ten-year prison sentence. When the bishop's body was returned to his family, it seemed to bear marks of torture. Pictures of his bruised body were widely circulated throughout the Catholic communities of China.[32]

For the underground Church, however, such evidence of brutality is not necessarily intimidating. Word of Bishop Fan's death served as a rallying cry for the underground Catholics of Hebei. The government imposed martial law on all the villages in the four Catholic dioceses of Hebei to prevent Catholics from gathering for a large funeral. Nonetheless, ten thousand Catholics attended.[33]

The underground movement has thus taken on a life of its own. It has been impossible for the Vatican to monitor the increasing numbers of underground bishops and priests. In some places, the underground Church has ordained an excessive number of bishops on the grounds that extra bishops are needed to ensure replacements if the principal bishop is arrested. Also, perhaps, underground bishops have succumbed to the psychological pressure to reward priests who were willing to risk martyrdom by conferring on them the status of bishop. In at least one diocese, it is rumored that nearly every underground priest is a bishop. Sometimes these bishops start fighting with each other, leading to confusion on the part of ordinary Catholics about who is in charge of their Church. Some of the underground clergy split into factions, and some have developed their own independent agendas, which might have to do as much with maximizing their own power as with benefiting the Church as a whole.[34] To further complicate matters, both the public Church and the underground Church are widely assumed by Chinese Catholics to be infiltrated by the secret police, who sometimes act as agents provocateurs. Using a colorful Chinese idiom, a Chinese Jesuit with contacts among both public and underground Catholics said that the underground Church and the public Church were "godly and diabolical" (*you shen, you gui*) at the same time. As time goes on, it becomes less clear whether any particular underground bishop or priest is a more legitimate Church authority than one who is now working aboveground.

If the Vatican had normal diplomatic relations with China, it could send a papal nuncio to China, and this nuncio could authoritatively adjudicate disputes over who should be the legitimate bishop in particular dioceses. That way, many Catholics would probably hate the nuncio in-

stead of hating each other, as they do now. But the normalization of relations with China would require that the Vatican break diplomatic relations with Taiwan, which it is reluctant to do because bishops on Taiwan might consider it a betrayal. Even more serious is the possibility
that China's underground priests would see it as a betrayal—a negation
of all the grievous sacrifices they have made as martyrs for the faith.
Some of the underground priests, says a European Jesuit social scientist
who has had some contact with them, are so invested with the identity
of hunted martyrs that (like the Mexican "whiskey priest" in Graham
Greene's *The Power and the Glory*) they could not stand the idea of living a routine aboveground life managing a normal parish—nor would
they have the skills to do so.

THE BITTER FRUIT OF HIERARCHICAL AMBIGUITY: THE CASE OF TIANJIN

There has thus been a severe blurring of the Church's legitimate authority structure—a critical flaw in a hierarchical community. The result
has been bitter conflict, such as the one I witnessed during my fieldwork
in Tianjin. For two decades, the Tianjin diocese had been formally governed by a bishop who had been associated with the founding of the
Chinese Catholic Patriotic Association, and as a result he was widely
despised by the Catholics of the diocese. His credibility was so low that
by the late 1980s he did not even live in Tianjin. With such a common
enemy, the Catholics in Tianjin achieved a high degree of unity.

A visitor to the Tianjin cathedral in the mid-1980s tells an anecdote
that illustrates this unity. He attended an early morning Mass celebrated
by a priest who had never accepted the Chinese Catholic Patriotic Association, had suffered for his resistance, but was now being allowed
by the government to resume his priestly functions. The Mass was
crowded. After the first priest finished, another priest came out to begin
a second Mass. All at once, with almost military precision, the whole
congregation stood up, turned their backs to the altar, and with a loud
stamping sound walked out of the church. The second priest, the visitor
later found, was called "Father Unbeliever" by the Tianjin Catholics
and was widely despised because of his collaboration with the government. Under these circumstances, a Catholic underground flourished.

In the early 1980s, Bishop Liu Shuhe, a longtime underground bishop
based in Yixian in Hebei, secretly consecrated Li Side bishop of Tianjin.
Bishop Li in turn secretly consecrated Bishop Shi Hongchen, an under-

ground priest who had spent from 1972 to 1979 in prison for illicitly
performing religious services in a public park. Later he also consecrated
Bishop Shi Hongzhen, a cousin of Shi Hongchen. In 1991, the official
bishop of Tianjin died. Alarmed perhaps by the Catholics' hostility toward the government-approved Church leadership, the Chinese Catholic Patriotic Association indicated that it would be willing to accept one
of the underground bishops as the official leader of the Tianjin diocese.
Its acceptance dropped an apple of discord into the Tianjin Church.

Each of the three underground bishops wanted to be the "Ordinary"—the official leader of the Tianjin diocese. Bishop Li Side, who
had consecrated the other two underground bishops, had a claim based
on seniority. But because of his confrontational nature, he was unacceptable to the government's Religious Affairs Bureau. Bishop Shi Hongchen
was willing to step forward, and, with the approval of the Religious Affairs Bureau and the Chinese Catholic Patriotic Association, he was in-
stalled as the official bishop of Tianjin in July 1992. The installation
ceremony was not a consecration, a ceremony in which an ordinary
priest is sacramentally given the status of a bishop. Those who supervised the arrangement of the ceremony—which had to include the Religious Affairs Bureau and Chinese Catholic Patriotic Association—were
thus willing to recognize Shi Hongchen as having already been validly
made a bishop even though his consecration had been performed by a
renegade, underground bishop whom the government deemed unable
to be Tianjin's spiritual leader.[35]

Bishop Shi's installation provoked a bitter split in the Tianjin Catholic community. Afraid that Bishop Li Side would foment unrest during
the installation of Bishop Shi, the government arrested him in the spring
of 1992 and kept him in detention during the installation ceremony. A
crowd of underground Catholics began to gather in the cathedral's courtyard, refusing to enter the church during the Mass. I had wandered into
this supercharged atmosphere on that feast of the Assumption in August 1992, only a month after Bishop Shi's controversial installation.

Later in the year, Bishop Li was released from prison and sent to
work in a remote country parish in Jixian, the suburban county farthest
away from Tianjin city. From there he continued to send secret messages to his followers. In a mimeographed pamphlet written on Pentecost 1993, he claimed that the Tianjin diocese had problems because
believers were lax and failed to manifest Jesus's spirit of sacrifice. Because
they were lax, they were too willing to compromise on matters of principle. But there could be absolutely no compromise with Shi Hongchen

and the public Church. This was a "line question," a question of whether one truly believed in Jesus. He went so far as to conclude that the diocese was in a state of schism. "The reason that the Tianjin diocese is now in a state of schism is not because two people have gone in opposite directions. We have not budged. It is the others who have left Holy Mother Church. . . . Only if they return to Holy Mother Church can we talk to them." The struggle over this matter of principle, he continued, would not weaken but would temper the Church and strengthen it in the long run. Others were arguing that compromises with the political authorities were necessary in order to gain freedom to spread the faith. But God demands above all that people be faithful to him. If they are, then God in his own way will assure that the faith is spread. "The Church of Christ was founded on the cross. Its distinctive characteristic has always been suffering. Our Chinese Church is not afraid of any suffering. . . . We hope that Catholics from overseas, if they truly want to support us, will not say much about things they don't clearly understand. Otherwise, they will simply make the situation more and more confused. . . . People say that we are too quarrelsome, too stubborn. But since this is a matter of principle, we have to be stubborn. Otherwise all of the suffering we have endured, all the years in prison, would have been for naught. . . . We have to mutually understand one another, but we absolutely cannot be ambiguous about a question of principle."

The document drew not only on the European spirit of martyrdom propagated by nineteenth-century missionaries but on the Chinese spirit of heroic self-sacrifice propagated by the Maoists during the Cultural Revolution. It was the Maoists who talked about "line struggles," about the inability to compromise on matters of principle, about the need to "temper oneself" through struggle. The defiant spirit of the underground Church thus blends European Christian asceticism with Maoist revolutionary asceticism.[36]

In response to Bishop Li's message, the official Church issued a mimeographed document of its own, more elegantly written and better printed than Bishop Li's. "For some time," the document said, "there have been circulating a number of preposterous allegations that have to varying degrees been troubling some of our good-hearted brothers and sisters. As a result some are having a hard time distinguishing fact from fiction, and their consciences are not at peace, to the point where they don't dare to enter the church, to attend Mass, receive Holy Communion—and saddest of all aren't able to receive the last rites when dying." To clarify the issues and calm the consciences of believers, the document cited a number of papal statements indicating that the pope considered the public Church in China to be connected with the universal Church, not to be in a state of schism from it. Where Bishop Li's statement was passionate and drew its rhetorical power from his witness of suffering, the public Church's document was somewhat dry and legalistic. It interpreted typically ambiguous papal statements in a light favorable to the public Church. For Bishop Li and his close followers, however, the issue was surely one of the spirit rather than the law—not about legal reasoning but about passionate commitment maintained in the face of suffering.

THE LIABILITIES OF HIERARCHY IN AMBIGUOUS TIMES

One of the strengths of the Chinese Catholic community, then, has been its hierarchical imagination. The Catholic ability to see grassroots communities as subordinate parts of a centrally ordered institution resonates with traditional Chinese ways of understanding the relation between social parts and a social whole, and it has given Chinese Catholics a way to transcend traditional, narrow loyalties to family, lineage, and region. But this strength becomes a grave weakness when a community actually has to be governed by a hierarchy and there is no unambiguous way to determine who ought to have various levels of authority within that hierarchy.

For now, Chinese Catholics have a strong cultural need for hierarchy without the means to create an unambiguous vertical chain of authority. Under these circumstances, the increasing ability of Catholics to develop strong horizontal bonds of solidarity leads to bitter factionalism as different local communities rally around different claimants to ecclesiastical authority. In parts of northern China, this factionalism has led to violent clashes between different Catholic villages or neighborhoods. The most gruesome tragedy arising from this atmosphere of fratricidal conflict so far has been the 1992 murder in Henan of a priest connected with the open Church by a disgruntled Catholic seminarian claiming that he was denied ordination because of his associations with the underground. He committed the crime by putting poison in the priest's chalice. The priest collapsed and died during Mass after drinking what he believed to be the Blood of Christ.[37]

The intensity of Catholic factionalism varies in different regions. In general, it is more intense in north China than in the south. Two main factors seem to account for this difference. The first is the density of local

Catholic populations. North China has the greatest concentrations of Catholics—indeed whole villages and even whole counties are Catholic. In those parts of south China where Catholic factionalism is relatively mild, Catholic communities are smaller and more scattered. Such communities, it seems, do not have the resources to mobilize themselves against other Catholics.

The second factor is the strength of authority structures. In the north legitimate claims to authority within the Church seem to be less clear than in the south. The closer one gets to Beijing, the more Religious Affairs Bureaus seem intent on interfering with the affairs of the Church, making it less likely that a diocese will have a bishop who will both be widely known to be approved by the Vatican and be able to function as an official bishop in the open Church. In south China, however, the Religious Affairs Bureaus, like most other government agencies, are more likely to be corrupt. As one Hong Kong–based scholar who is closely involved with the Church in China put it, such Religious Affairs officials love money more than they hate religion. Some well-placed bribes will help them look the other way when local Catholics install a bishop who has been quietly approved by Rome. With a bishop who is widely perceived as legitimate, there is less of a basis for factions to develop. In some places, the public Church and the underground Church even amicably share the same church building.[38]

The more difficult it is to establish an ecclesiastical authority structure that would be unambiguously legitimate in the eyes of most Catholics, the more the Chinese Catholic Church is plagued by division. Under such circumstances, the very social forces that have increased the solidarity within particular Catholic communities increase the conflicts among communities. Creating a civil society in China's present circumstances— "soft," transitional times—requires communities that can function effectively in a situation full of "uncertainty, ambiguity, opacity, and confusion."[39] Insofar as it remains imbued with its rather rigid, pre–Vatican II understanding of hierarchy, the Chinese Catholic Church may have difficulty making a constructive contribution under such circumstances to a Chinese civil society.

CHAPTER TWO

Community and Solidarity

If Saint Augustine had been writing about the Chinese Catholic Church, he might have entitled his masterwork *The Village of God*, rather than *The City of God*. Once Catholic missionaries lost all contact with the Qing literati because of the outcome of the Rites Controversy, they had to confine most of their proselytizing to the countryside. In time they rationalized that rural people naturally made better Catholics because, as a Maryknoll missionary put it in the early twentieth century, they were unaffected by the urban temptations of "Venus and Mammon."[1] This strong rural bias heavily influences the mentality of Chinese Catholics to this day. One could conservatively estimate that at least 80 percent of Chinese Catholics live in rural communities.[2]

For reasons mentioned in the previous chapter, missionaries aimed to convert not individuals but whole communities—whole villages or at least whole segments of villages. As Owen Lattimore colorfully remarked in the course of describing a Catholic missionary compound in the 1920s, Catholic missions were based on "radically different principles and practice" from Protestant missions. "The Catholics begin with the land, which is the heart of the Chinese people, and aim less at the soul of the individual than at the life of the community. The principle seems to be that if you build up a Catholic community, family by family, grounded on the Church, instead of gathering a lot of stray sheep, here a son and there a brother and there a grandmother, then the individual in the community will have the same chances of Heaven, Hell, or Purgatory as the individual in a Catholic community in Europe or America."[3]

Thus, in the countryside, the forms of Catholic community life blend together with the common social forms of Chinese village life.[4] Sociologically, Catholic villages appear similar to ordinary non-Catholic ones. There are the same kinds of lineage organization, in which whole villages or whole segments of villages claim descent from a single common ancestor. There are the same patterns of economic activities and the same political structures. And there are the same kinds of collective memories of land reform, collectivization, the Great Leap Forward, the Cultural Revolution, and, finally, in the 1980s, decollectivization. The main obvious differences are in the use of religious symbols. The Catholics have churches rather than temples; in their houses they hang pictures of the Blessed Virgin rather than of folk deities.

There are more subtle differences, however. In the words of a young college-educated man who left his village and his faith but still keeps in close touch with his family home, "Catholics are better organized." In Catholic regions, many villages have been rebuilding church buildings destroyed as the result of former antireligious policies. But, in many parts of China, the neighboring non-Catholic villages are not rebuilding their temples. This discrepancy is not the result of non-Catholic villages' giving up all religion—on the contrary, folk-religious practices have been mushrooming since the 1980s—but it is the result of Catholic villages' superior ability to marshal the collective resources needed to rebuild churches.[5] This is the case even when Catholic villages are poorer than their non-Catholic neighbors. According to reports from "the Public Security Bureau and the Religious Affairs Bureau," cited by a team of researchers from Beijing University in the mid-1980s, Catholic villages, in Shanxi Province at least, are less prone to crime, more harmonious, and more efficient in farm work than are non-Catholic villages. As the Beijing University researchers described one village, its "Catholics have a very strong feeling that 'all Catholics under heaven are a single family.'"[6]

Yet, from the point of view of the government, internal harmony sometimes has a negative aspect. Somewhat contradicting its portrait of strong mutual commitment, the Beijing University report states that "the biggest shortcoming of these Catholics is their selfishness, their lack of public spirit. They take advantage of the collective and harm public property. When Catholics see such a thing happening, they don't do anything about it; when they know about it they don't report it, but instead they cover up for one another. They think that they would rather say the rosary and attend Mass than take care of such matters. They are a strong centrifugal force. They often get together and collectively resist their proper work." In the village study on which these conclusions are based, the Beijing researchers claim that the Catholics managed to resist paying their irrigation bills with the help of the village accountant, who apparently was a Catholic himself. Although Catholics will do anything for the Church, the report continues, they will not contribute to collective road-repair projects. And they will not go to political meetings but will eagerly attend church.[7]

In this place at least, the villagers had a strong enough public life, but it was opposed to what the government considered the only true public realm. Moreover, Catholic solidarity was closely connected with a positively belligerent attitude toward government officials. When one villager renounced his faith to join the Communist Party, villagers pelted him with rocks. When teams from the county government arrived in 1985 to carry out family-planning policies, they were surrounded by crowds of angry villagers, and when they retreated to their living quarters, rocks were thrown through their windows. They did not dare go out at night. Finally they had to be rescued by a team of police.[8]

Other Catholic villages, however, maintain a high degree of solidarity without so much belligerence. In another Catholic village studied by the Beijing University team, a village in the same province but in a different county, the Catholics have built an impressive new church, which is well attended. These villagers are considerably more cooperative with local officials. The researchers say that this cooperation is the result of the local Communist Party officials' treating Catholics the same as non-Catholics in this area, even during the Maoist era.[9] In contrast, in the previously mentioned village, the Party made a major effort to destroy the Catholic community. They even put extra pressure on Catholics not to have many children while encouraging non-Catholics to have extra children. These tactics intensified Catholics' commitment to their faith and encouraged them to identify that faith with a spirit of resistance. In the village that received more evenhanded treatment, Catholics did not connect their faith with hostility toward government authorities.[10]

Such evidence indicates that Catholic villages generally possess above-average community solidarity, which is based on a spirit of "generalized reciprocity," the willingness of Catholics to come to each other's aid and to work together on common projects. The pattern observed by Lattimore in the 1920s continues in the 1990s. "The jealousy that Chinese have toward Catholic communities is directed at something different [than the "foreignness" associated with Protestants]—at their solidarity and self-sufficiency. This very jealousy would, in the absence of foreign support, tend to hold Catholic communities together by the strength of outside pressure, confirming the strength of family ties and property interests into which the religious principle has been interwoven." [11]

But the solidarity of Catholic communities varies in quality as well as quantity. In some places the solidarity is belligerent, built on resentment of outsiders, especially government officials. In other places the solidarity is relatively irenic, based on a spirit of cooperation that can lead Catholics not only to help themselves but to work with various non-Catholics to improve society. In our attempt to ascertain whether Catholic social relations are of the kind that could support a civil society, let us now examine in detail the sources of Catholic village solidarity and then determine those factors that make some kinds of solidarity more or less belligerent.

CATHOLICISM AS ETHNICITY

Rural Catholicism is less a chosen faith than an ascribed status. To be a Catholic, say all of the rural people whom we interviewed, is first and foremost to believe in the "God Teachings" (*xin Tianzhu jiao*). But, in practice, this is not a matter so much of personal faith as of inherited membership in a community. Its religious principle interwoven with "family ties and property interests," a Chinese rural Catholic community is formed by bonds that for most practical purposes cannot be broken unless one leaves the countryside. When one has an identity that one cannot discard, even if one wants to, and one is persecuted or discriminated against because of this identity, then one's consciousness of that identity and one's commitment to communities that share that identity become strong. Community ties are not weakened but confirmed by "the strength of outside pressure."

Chinese Catholicism, in short, is a kind of ethnicity.[12] It is not so classified in the official Chinese categorization, which distinguishes between "ethnic groups" (*minzu*—also translated "nationalities") like Islam and "religions" (*zongjiao*) like Catholicism.[13] Nonetheless, several Chinese intellectuals, including a Chinese Muslim (*Hui*) who was connected with the Religious Affairs Bureau, remarked to me that, sociologically, the Catholic communities I studied had a relationship to their faith and to outsiders similar to that of *Hui* communities in the same area. In China, however, an ethnic group is more a political than a sociological designation. The term is used for fifty-five relatively large populations (Muslims, Tibetans, Mongols, Manchus) and small populations (out of hundreds of groups that applied for the designation) that have distinctive languages, cultures, or religious beliefs, and whose support has been strategically important for the Chinese regime. Groups that are so designated get special privileges, like exemption from the one-child policy, a certain amount of local autonomy, and some "affirmative action" in admission to higher education. Catholics would never have applied for this status because they did not want to set themselves apart as culturally different from other Chinese; and they would never have been designated an ethnic group and given the privileges that come with it because they have been of no strategic value to the Chinese government.

In their social practices, however, Catholics act like an ethnic group and have done so all the more since being persecuted under the Maoist regime and discriminated against during the Deng Xiaoping regime. To better understand the consequences, let us examine in detail how rural Catholicism functions as an ethnicity, even though members and outsiders alike say it is a religious faith. Although Catholics define themselves as people who believe in the God Teachings, as distinguished from most non-Catholics, who believe simply in the Big Teaching (*xin da jiao*)—that is, rural Chinese folk religion—they in practice consider as Catholics people who seem basically agnostic. They distinguish between the "true believers" (*xinde zhen*) and the "indifferent" (*lengdan*, literally "cold and weak"). The extremely indifferent never set foot inside a church, never pray, and profess skepticism about all Catholic doctrines. Yet, as one rural Catholic priest said, "even if a person is an indifferent believer, there is still a place for God in his heart." Few Catholics except those who have to formally renounce the faith in order to join the Communist Party ever completely leave the Church.

Even the extremely indifferent participate in the one ritual that distinguishes them from all non-Catholics—Catholic funerals. Virtually all rural Catholics bury their dead in a way that is similar to yet distinct from that of non-Catholic peasants. Like those of the Big Teaching, Catholic funerals are elaborate, day-long affairs, involving enclosure of the body in a large wooden casket, a banquet for extended family, and a long procession of relatives wearing white burlap mourning garments and arrayed in order of their blood relationship; the procession to the grave site is accompanied by shrill music from traditional wind instruments and the wailing of professional mourners. If a priest is available, he attends the funeral and leads its prayers. But like non-Catholic rural funerals, the event is organized mainly by the deceased's family.

What distinguishes God Teaching from Big Teaching funeral rituals is that the family members do not kowtow to the casket, do not burn incense sticks and mock paper money, and do not set out offerings of food at the grave site. These are the rituals of "ancestor worship" that were the objects of the Rites Controversy; they were permitted by Jesuit missionaries in the seventeenth century but proscribed in the early eighteenth century by Pope Clement XI. Instead of performing these forbidden rites, Catholic peasants sprinkle holy water on the casket and say prayers for the dead. On the burial mounds or tombstones, instead of the little platform on which non-Catholics place offerings of food, there is often a simple cross.

Even those who were born into a Catholic family but are now skeptical of all Catholic doctrines, never go to Church, and never pray will give a Catholic funeral to their parents. The alternative to a Catholic funeral is not a Big Teaching funeral but a purely secular one. During the Cultural Revolution, China's peasants were forced to have secular memorial services, but they resented it, and as soon as restrictions were lifted in the late 1970s, they resumed their traditional rituals. Today, Communist Party members are theoretically supposed to receive a secular, a-religious funeral, but even they usually do not. Rural Chinese funerals symbolize the bonds of kinship that are central to rural life: they connect families to preceding generations and offer hope to generations yet to come. For a peasant (Catholic or non-Catholic) to be bereft of such connections is to be not only lonely but vulnerable, cut off from the primary claims to loyalty necessary to carry on cooperative enterprises and to secure protection against hostile strangers.[14] When Catholics die, the family has to symbolize this sense of connection in a ritual language common to almost all the relatives and common to the ancestors who recently preceded them. The only such language is the Catholic variant of folk death ritual.

If people have grown up Catholic and live in a Catholic family, they cannot avoid using Catholic ceremonies to express their social identity—their membership in a particular family and lineage—even if they do not believe the tenets of the Catholic faith. As long as they need such membership, which they will need as long as they live and work close to their rural home, they retain a Catholic identity. If they do not need such membership, as might be the case if they move to a city and join the Communist Party, they can give up their Catholic identity. But, as acknowledged by a middle-aged official who had done just that, "according to the Catholic custom, if a Catholic renounces the faith, it is just like dying."

The necessity of being buried as a Catholic makes it important to marry as one. Almost all the Catholic villagers we interviewed agreed that, all things being equal, it was preferable for Catholics to seek Catholic wives (whether true believer or indifferent did not especially matter) for their sons. Says a true-believing Catholic peasant woman in her late twenties, "Catholics must get married to Catholics because they have the same religious beliefs. Even if they are not true believers, they can come together for common festivals, like funerals and marriages." We met some young women who had traveled about six hundred miles from Harbin, in China's northeast, to Xian County in Hebei Province because they could not find suitable Catholic marriage partners in their home regions. "Nobody stops a Catholic from marrying a non-Catholic," says a Xian County father of a nun and a seminarian, as well as a married elder son. "But you have to be careful; it's best not to do it. In my village it is possible to find somebody of the same religion, but in a big city it is not possible. So I tolerate mixed marriages. But in my village almost everybody is married to a Catholic."

Clearly, for some rural Catholics, the God Teaching is a genuine faith. They believe the doctrines and use them to give meaning to their personal experience. They are committed to praying regularly and to receiving the sacraments. They are willing to suffer for their beliefs. Whether or not they genuinely believe its teachings, however, for most rural Catholics their religion is a status, inherited from their parents, that they cannot cast aside even if they wanted to. As the middle-aged wife of a Catholic village leader puts it, "No Catholics can renounce their faith even though, in hard times, under pressure of politics, they say they don't believe anymore. A person may be an indifferent Catholic and not good at following the rules of the Church. But he will never betray the faith." All of which fits the classic sociological definition of an ethnic identity.

REPRESSION AND COMMUNITY SOLIDARITY

During the Maoist era, as we have seen, the government harshly persecuted Catholics. It imprisoned many of their priests and tried to replace them with priests who appeared to renounce Catholic orthodoxy and to defy the express wishes of the pope for the sake of collaborating with the new government. The government itself barraged villagers with atheistic propaganda. Especially during the Cultural Revolution, Red Guards destroyed village churches and harshly punished any open practice of the faith. If Catholicism had been purely a matter of individual religious faith, one would have expected the Catholic community to be decimated. The "lukewarm" would have wanted to avoid persecution by renouncing their lightly held belief. By all accounts, including accounts of Catholic missionaries themselves, many Catholics before 1949 were indeed lukewarm, no more than "rice Christians." Undoubtedly, the Maoist government assumed that it could easily drive these lukewarm Catholics out of the Church, leaving only a relatively small core of true believers who could be isolated and if necessary imprisoned or executed. But since rural Catholicism was an identity that could not be discarded at will, outside pressure only confirmed that quasi-ethnic identity and infused it with resentment against the government.

Bereft of the guidance of their priests, Catholics learned to organize themselves. Parents and grandparents gave newborn infants a "provisional baptism" (daixi) by pouring a little water over the child's head and uttering the ritual formula, "I baptize thee in the name of the Father, the Son, and the Holy Ghost." Grandmothers especially carried out these sacramental rituals, following traditional patterns in which elderly women were responsible for the ritual life of their families but also taking advantage of the fact that elderly women were more likely than others to get away with proscribed activities during the Maoist era. Grandmothers, too, most often carried out the work of religious instruction, teaching their grandchildren to memorize the basic prayers, the Ten Commandments, and some of the main doctrines from the catechism. Catholics of all ages continued to say the rosary by murmuring the prayers and counting them out on their fingers with their hands in their pockets. Since they had been instructed that it was better to pray in common than alone, they sometimes met in small groups to say the rosary in someone's darkened house. This was risky since any unapproved group activity was especially severely punished by the government. To organize such groups successfully required courage, initiative, and considerable interpersonal skills. Doing such work constituted an education in how to carry out clandestine activity in a repressive society.

Sometimes the leaders of such groups were caught and punished. Especially during the Cultural Revolution, Red Guards targeted all such informal leaders. Some were tortured in the hope that they would renounce the faith; and if they did not, they were subjected to public "struggle sessions" in an attempt to destroy their influence among the people. Those who survived were eventually revered as martyrs and had more influence than ever.

The attitude of lax Catholics toward such martyrs is perhaps typical of the way, through persecution, even Catholics who were not true believers nonetheless deepened their Catholic identity. Lax Catholics speak of their Church's martyrs with great respect. Even though they themselves would not have followed the path to martyrdom, they admire the martyrs for their integrity under pressure—for standing up for something that was important even to lax Catholics, for a part of their identity that, even if they could not firmly believe it belonged to God, at least did not belong to the state.

In short, the years of persecution deepened Catholics' understanding of themselves as a quasi-ethnic community, gave them experience in organizing their own religious activities, even in defiance of the government, and created a proving ground for informal lay leadership. Often, under the missionaries, Catholic laypeople had been relatively passive. Communities were organized vertically, with authority in the hands of the priest and his paid catechists.[15] Now communities were increasingly organized horizontally. True believers took an active role in organizing these communities, and even the lax found themselves more invested in a Catholic identity than before.

This growing Catholic solidarity was kept from overtly manifesting itself by the raw power of the state. But when the repression lifted in the early 1980s, this hard-won solidarity blossomed into practice. Informal lay leaders helped to reorganize their communities. As analyzed in a study by a sociologist at Beijing University, these lay leaders (*huizhang*) are people who, first, have a lot of "symbolic capital" from connections with old Catholic families that often include priests and nuns; second, usually have a lot of organizational ability; and, third, sometimes have access to material resources that can be used to benefit the Church.[16]

One goal of the new Catholic activism was the recovery of Church property and the rebuilding of churches. "When our Church was torn down [during the Cultural Revolution]," recalls Mr. Li, a lay leader in one of the villages we visited, "I took the rafters and brought them into my house. And I swore that one day I would rebuild that church." In the mid-eighties, he got his opportunity. He organized community dinners at which villagers pledged money for reconstruction. A small amount of money came from the government, in compensation for some of the property that had been destroyed. A larger sum of money was contributed by Catholics outside China, probably (he was deliberately vague about the exact source of the money) from Chinese Catholics in Taiwan, Hong Kong, or the Philippines who had escaped from the region around the village when the Communists took power. Even the relatively lax often joined in these building efforts. Contributing was an expression not so much of an internalized religious faith as of loyalty to their local community. Where they did not have government permission or local resources to build a church, they erected large canopies under which Mass could be said.

Since there was now a shortage of clergy, most villages had Mass only during periodic visits of a priest. But every morning and evening, the most pious among the faithful gathered for prayer, sometimes at the sound of a bell pealing from the church steeple. On Sunday, even when a priest was not present, the churches filled with villagers gathering for common prayer led by one of the lay leaders. When a priest did come, the churches were even more full. And, on special feast days, like Christmas, Easter, and the Assumption of Mary, even many of the lax Catholics turned out, flowing out of the small churches into the surrounding courtyards.

Moreover, the emergence of lay leaders represented a democratic impulse whose genuineness contrasts with that of the village elections sponsored by the government. As noted by the Beijing University sociologist cited above, although Catholic lay leaders are formally elected to their positions, "the election (as one villager put it) doesn't make much difference because the same persons who were in charge before the election are in charge after it." "Compared with elections to the village governance committee," however, "these elections are much more democratic. Although both kinds of elections are foregone conclusions, those chosen to be Catholic leaders are truly people who have high prestige and ability. . . . They really do represent the will of the people. . . . Although the village governance committee is officially elected, its members are basically appointed from above, and their election is just a formality. Their prestige is lower than that of the Catholic leaders." [17]

Under such conditions, the local church has become the center of a strong, active community, bolstered by pride in accomplishing, under indigenous leadership, projects that had long been forbidden and are now, at best, only reluctantly permitted by the state. Church property cannot be recovered and churches cannot be rebuilt, however, without some cooperation from the government's Religious Affairs Bureau. Whether by necessity or by manipulative design, the government has not returned every village's Catholic property or allowed every Catholic community to rebuild its church. In some regions, this discrepancy has set in motion bitter conflicts among Catholic communities.

SOLIDARITY AND ANIMOSITY

The community spirit that was generated once repression was lifted centered around hopes for rebuilding churches and returning to what villagers remembered as a normal Catholic life. Though suspicious of the government, most communities were happy enough to take back from the government the property they thought had been stolen and happy to receive permission to rebuild their churches. But a village that did not get this permission could become extremely jealous of a neighbor that did. Sometimes, jealous people in the deprived village might spread the rumor that the successful village had compromised its faith by working too closely with the Religious Affairs Bureau. The deprived village might put up its canopy and carry out its prayer services in defiance of government regulations and claim that its faith was all the purer for this act. Forged in a crucible of resistance, the solidarity of local Catholic communities could thus make them suspicious of one another as well as of the government.[18]

Under certain circumstances, these suspicions can sour into bitter animosity. Sometimes, Catholic communities display even more hostility toward one another than toward the government. Their leaders declare rival communities to be excommunicated and to be inhabited by the devil. There are reports of violent battles waged by rural Catholic communities against each other in Shandong Province. These battles are sometimes reported as clashes between the "official" Church and the "underground" Church, but this characterization is misleading. First, none of the communities involved in such conflicts are clandestine. Some have not received any patronage from the Religious Affairs Bureau and may be carrying out religious activities without permission from the government or the approval of the Chinese Catholic Patriotic Association. But everybody in the local area, including the local officials, knows what is going on. Such an "underground" operates very much in the light of day.[19]

Second, and more important, battles between local Catholic commu-

Figure 5. Unregistered chapel inside a rural house. Photograph by Richard Madsen.

nities are not particular instances of a more general conflict between two different national Catholic communities united around different conceptions of fealty to the Holy See. In some places, communities labeled "underground" get along quite amicably with communities considered "official." In Fujian Province, an officially recognized Catholic community has helped an "underground" community build a new church.[20] The difference between "official" and "underground" Catholic communities is more political than theological: the official communities have the approval of the local Religious Affairs Bureau for rebuilding or reopening a church and for carrying out religious activities, while the underground communities have no such approval. Conflict between official and unofficial Catholic communities is not general or inevitable.

Strong community conflicts are likely to erupt where resources are scarce and Religious Affairs Bureaus are the sole conduits for supplying them, which is especially the case in north China. Where resources are more abundant, as is often the case in south China, where the economy is in general stronger, and where there are more channels for foreign religious societies to send money to local communities, there is less reason for strong animosity to develop between officially approved and unofficial communities.

Where animosity does develop, however, it is intensified by the ambiguity that presently exists in many places about who is a legitimate bishop and about the permissible level of cooperation with state authorities. Traditionally, the Catholic Church's parochial communities have been joined into a universal community of communities by the hierarchy. When the hierarchy is in disarray, particularism reigns. The ambiguities concerning legitimate ecclesiastical authority that plague some parts of Catholic China allow leaders in rival communities to make claims of righteousness and to consign their opponents to the devil. Where there is less ambiguity, as when the officially approved local bishop is widely known to be approved by the Vatican, there is less conflict, even though some communities benefit from official government approval and others do not.[21]

As I have described it so far, the connection between Catholic community solidarity and animosity toward the government or toward other Catholic communities is more a matter of sociology than of theology. It is what happens when a government attempts to suppress an insuppressible ethnic identity and what happens after the suppression is lifted and different communities have unequal opportunities to assert their identity. But the connection between solidarity and animosity is also related to certain aspects of Catholic theology—not the theology inscribed in the gospels, with their injunction to "love your enemies and do good to those who hate you," but that communicated through the traditions still handed down within Chinese Catholic villages.

Based on the Constantinian theology of Christendom, these traditions teach Chinese Catholics that the ideal society is one in which religion controls all social institutions. In medieval Christendom, the Church legitimated the political authorities, often dominated the economy, controlled the schools, and was the chief source of help for the poor and sick. Although the Church lost comprehensive control of such institutions after the Reformation, up until the second Vatican Council, most of its leaders still saw it as their sacred mission to regain as much of such control as possible. Where Catholics were a minority of the population, as in China, they sought to exert such control through the creation of enclaves dominated by the Church. Thus, to be a Catholic, say the local community leaders whom we interviewed in Xian County, is to live in "the world of God."

This is a self-enclosed world. In many Catholic communities before the Communists took power, elementary education took place in

Church-run schools, health care was provided by a Catholic clinic, and economic aid in time of disaster was provided by Church-dispensed charity. Local political leaders were Catholics. Social life revolved around the church, and Catholic festivals were the most important community activities. As a Maryknoll missionary remembers, "There was a bell to assemble the Catholics to recite the Angelus, morning and evening prayers. The sound of the bell could reach as much as five or six miles. Upon hearing the bell, Catholics working in the fields would recite the Angelus, and on Sunday would come to hear Mass."[22] True believers still believe that they should try to re-create this world.

For example, one of the local Catholic leaders we interviewed—a layman who led the drive to rebuild his village's church—tells of receiving his vocation in an apparition that sounds like the famous vision of the Emperor Constantine.

> One night, [during the anti-Japanese war], I went out to water my draught animals. Suddenly, I saw a meteor, just like a fire in the sky. At that time [in spite of growing up in a Catholic family], I didn't believe in God; I was in school and was following Darwin's theory that man evolved from monkeys. But the meteor was in the shape of a cross, burning a great fire. There were a lot of people watering their animals together with me, but I was the only one who saw the fire. I didn't know what it was. I felt confused. Then I came home and asked my grandfather, who had been wounded during the Boxer uprising. He told me, "This means that you should follow the rules of the Church. Someday, religious trials are going to befall you. I will not be around to face these trials, but you certainly will."

This lay leader thinks his life has fulfilled the prophecy of the burning cross. In the 1950s, the Communists sentenced him to fifteen years in prison because he had played a leadership role in his Catholic community; but his time in prison only strengthened and deepened his faith.

Even when they have not received Constantinian visions, most of the rural true believers whom we interviewed dedicate themselves to making their village a miniature Christendom, a self-enclosed world of God. To do so, they have to convince themselves and their fellow Catholics that the outside world is evil and dangerous in order to encourage animosity toward it. So identified is the rural Catholic faith with this idea of a world of God that when Catholics adopt an accommodating attitude toward the non-Catholic world, they begin to lose their faith. They remain ethnic Catholics, but their belief and practice become lax. And their villages lose what they call their "strong Catholic atmosphere."

CATHOLIC COMMUNITY ATMOSPHERE

As a middle-aged man from a village with such an atmosphere puts it, "Because everybody lives in a Catholic atmosphere, it is not necessary to study something. They naturally know about the faith." In a village with a strong Catholic atmosphere, a large group attends morning and evening prayers, and the church is packed during Sunday Mass. Such a village produces a number of vocations to the priesthood or sisterhood. Most marriages of village men are to Catholic women, and the marriages are ratified in a ceremony by a priest before the wedding festivities (which in most other respects are the same as those in Big Teaching peasant villages). Few villagers join the Communist Party.[23]

In a village with a very weak Catholic atmosphere, attendance at common prayer will be sparse. There will be no vocations to the clergy and many mixed marriages. A relatively large number of Catholic villagers will have joined the Communist Party.

Villages that do not have a militant faith, deepened through the experience of persecution, tend to lose their Catholic atmosphere. As mentioned at the beginning of this chapter, a Beijing University research team noticed a significant difference in levels of belligerence between a village that had been severely harassed by local officials during the Maoist years and one that had received more lenient treatment. There was not a great difference in the strength of the internal Catholic atmosphere within the two communities. In both, the local church was well attended, and the rituals of Catholic life were actively carried out. Yet subtle changes were beginning to occur in the more accommodating community. Children did not attend daily prayers as much as in the more belligerent village; their parents encouraged them to stay home and finish their homework instead. In the more belligerent community, parents discouraged their children from taking school seriously since all the teachers were non-Catholic and the curriculum was considered by the parents to be atheistic and materialistic. But although parents in the more accommodating community might have been concerned about the content of the curriculum, they wanted their children to succeed. Similarly, the lure of worldly success was pulling some of the adults away from regular religious practice. Many of the families in the village had gotten involved in a thriving transport business, and the heads of these households were too busy making money to attend church regularly. (They reportedly rationalized by saying that they could best help the church by helping to make their village rich.) And while in the more belligerent village the Catholics refused to buy television sets for fear of moral decay, in the more accommodating village young and old alike were enjoying TV.[24]

These cases suggest that when faith is seen as a commitment to create a self-enclosed world of God, the strength of that faith depends on isolation from secular life. One way Chinese Catholics can protect their faith from the outside world is to maintain an active belligerence toward that world. When they do not, the faith still does not disappear as long as Catholics have relatively restricted opportunities for participating successfully in the wider world. But once the lure of success is present, it is hard to resist. So, even when local Catholic leaders have not been embittered by persecution, they may well feel a religious mission to stir up a militant attitude toward the outside world. In the long run, however, this attempt will probably be futile as long as the outside world truly beckons. Given the theological legacy and social structure of the Chinese Catholic Church, the greatest threat to Catholic devotion is not political pressure but social openness.

OPEN AND CLOSED COMMUNITIES

These hypotheses are borne out by our ethnographies of villages with strong and weak Catholic atmospheres in Hebei Province. (See Map 2 in the Introduction for the location of these villages.) The villages we found with the strongest Catholic atmosphere were in the Xian County area. Evangelized by Jesuits in the nineteenth century, Xian County is over 90 percent Catholic. It has a reputation for a staunch Catholic faith, and in our observation it lives up to that reputation. The Catholic center of the Xian County diocese is the market town of Zhangzhuang. Here the Jesuits built a large and famous cathedral, together with a hospital, orphanage, and seminary—all of which were destroyed or secularized during the Maoist era.[25] Since the beginning of the Deng Xiaoping regime, the Zhangzhuang cathedral has been rebuilt, a minor seminary has been reopened, a convent has been revived, and a Catholic clinic has been reestablished. On Christmas, the cathedral is packed with worshipers coming from throughout the surrounding area to keep vigil all night on Christmas eve and to attend morning Mass said by the bishop. But during ordinary times the cathedral is relatively empty. For all its glorious history, its splendid cathedral, and its concentration of priests and nuns, Zhangzhuang's Catholic atmosphere is considered more lax than that of some of the smaller villages surrounding it. In some of these villages, virtually the entire population attends Mass regularly, and most marry Catholics. Such villages provide one of the greatest sources of vocations in northern China. Compared with such villages, a relatively low percentage of Zhangzhuang's Catholics attend regular church services; there are more mixed marriages and not as high a rate of vocations.

Laxer still, we found, were the Catholic villages in Baodi County, which is part of the Tianjin Municipality (although about two hours by train from the city). Some villages in Baodi trace their faith back to the time of Matteo Ricci, but most, like those in Xian County, were evangelized in the nineteenth and early twentieth centuries. Unlike Xian County—but like most counties in China where Catholics are found—Baodi is mostly non-Catholic. Only about a third of its residents are Catholic. They are concentrated, however, in several districts of the county; and they belong to lineages that are mostly Catholic and usually live in villages that are mostly Catholic. Since the mid-1980s, the Catholic villages in Baodi County have erected some fine new churches. But although they are full on festivals like Christmas (even when the temperature is below freezing, some worshipers, bundled up in their thick jackets and scarves, can be found standing outside the packed church), on ordinary Sundays they are less than half full. (The churches have a seating capacity of about a hundred and are located in villages with a population of about a thousand.) And only a handful of elderly Catholics, mostly women, meet for daily morning and evening prayer.

In these villages there are a large number of mixed marriages. Even children from old Catholic families have joined the Communist Party. Although there are some elderly priests in Tianjin who have come from this region, there have been almost no recent vocations. In this region, true-believing Catholics themselves admit that their villages are lax.

The present differences between the Catholic atmospheres of Baodi and Xian Counties can be explained in terms of their social and economic openness. Consider first the economic situation of the regions. Xian County, which has perhaps the strongest concentration of Catholics in China, is officially designated a "poverty-stricken county." There is indeed a sense of economic depression in the region. Villagers still live in dark, drafty houses made of adobe brick with packed earth floors. Warmth in the winter is provided by the traditional heated brick platform, called a kang, which dominates the central room of the house and provides a sleeping place for all members of the family. At night, illumination comes from a single, small, incandescent light bulb. Although

Figure 6. Christmas midnight Mass in a village church. Photograph by Fan Lizhu.

Figure 7. Traditional musical instruments at midnight Mass. Photograph by Fan Lizhu.

most houses now have a Chinese-made black-and-white television, on which the residents watch snowy, flickering images of Chinese opera and traditional acrobatics, they do not usually have sewing machines or washing machines. Not even the adolescent villagers wear the bright clothing that is filling up city and township department stores.

The sense of economic backwardness extends to many of the public spaces of Xian County's communities. The dirt lanes that wind through the villages are strewn with garbage. Bridges over streams are rickety and lack safety handrails. The one exception to the decay afflicting public spaces is the churches. Most villages now have fine new brick and stucco churches decorated on the inside with bright pictures and statues of the Blessed Virgin, Jesus, and St. Joseph; the churches are kept clean and neat and are usually adorned with fresh flowers.

Xian County's economy is based almost entirely on agriculture. Today, however, the source of wealth in rural China is not agriculture—the profit from agriculture has been declining since the mid-1980s—but manufacturing industries, usually centered in townships. Xian County has almost no manufacturing industries. (The only significant commercial sidelines for villagers are traditional handicrafts, especially the making of paper flowers.) The lack of township industries is due partly to Xian County's remoteness and the poor quality of its transportation infrastructure. (There is no railroad link directly to Xian County; and the roads are narrow and prone to lengthy traffic jams.) But it is also due to political factors. Xian County remains a "closed" county. Foreigners need special permission to visit there, and the county is not allowed to seek outside commercial investment. Xian County is closed because of its strong concentration of Catholics. The government wants to keep outsiders away because it distrusts the county's Catholics and is afraid that they will be influenced by outside agitators.

The closed character of the county is deepened by its lack of a strong, indigenous Communist Party. Take, for instance, Liu Village, a single-surname village almost all of whose members belong to the same lineage and all of whom are Catholic. Not a single member of the Liu lineage is a member of the Communist Party. One outsider family in the village, named Yang, provides all the village's Communist Party members and therefore all its formal political leadership. The Communist Party here does not come from the people but is a small, alien force. Yet, Party membership provides the main connections necessary to bring government investment into a region. Without strong, locally rooted Party members, the Xian County region cannot attract investment capital.

Because the county is closed, the strength of the Catholic atmosphere in its villages is maintained. The county's main connection with outsiders is through the Catholic Church. After 1949, many priests and sisters from Xian County ended up in foreign countries like Taiwan and the Philippines. These native sons and daughters have been sending money back to the county not to build factories but to rebuild churches and other religious institutions. The county has become rich in institutions of worship, poor in institutions for economic development.

In contrast, Baodi County has many of the signs of China's new prosperity. One of the most striking indications of its relative standard of living is in the bride prices families must pay when they arrange a marriage for their sons. Whereas in Xian County they have to pay about four hundred yuan to the family of the bride, in Baodi they have to pay about four thousand yuan. Baodi's houses are new, made of sturdy bricks. Some of them have handsome facades of colored tile. Inside they are bright, with light streaming through glass windows. At night they benefit from fluorescent lights. Some houses have central heating through metal radiators, and instead of kangs they have Western-style beds, softened by spring mattresses. Most houses have late-model color television sets and a variety of modern household appliances, including propane stoves, refrigerators, and washing machines. Some of the houses are stuffed with kitschy knickknacks and decorated with colorful posters; in true-believer Catholic families, these posters are of Mary or Jesus, but, in the majority of lax families, they are of Disneyland or of women in bathing suits. The liveliest and most prosperous parts of the county are the market towns, which are mostly non-Catholic. But the Catholic villages have received at least some of the benefits of the general prosperity. The public infrastructure seems in good repair, especially when compared with that in Xian County. Roads are freshly paved, and village lanes are kept relatively clean. Scattered throughout the Catholic parts of the county are some handsome, newly built churches, although there are not as many as in Xian County, where almost every village has its church.

The area is not nearly as prosperous as Guangdong or Zhejiang Provinces; but it has undergone an impressive amount of economic growth since the mid-1980s and especially in the early 1990s. The growth is mostly due to a variety of township industries: factories for manufacturing textiles, plastic household utensils, and paper clips, and food-processing plants and a printing plant. The area has secured capital for these industries and markets for its products because of connections between its leaders and the city of Tianjin. It has also been aided by its relatively good transportation links with Tianjin.

There does seem to be a connection between the poverty of Xian County and the strong Catholic atmosphere of its villages and between the relative wealth of Baodi and the weak Catholic atmosphere of its villages. But the connection between poverty and faith is by no means a matter of simple cause and effect. If it were, the poorest villages would always have the strongest Catholic atmosphere, and the richest villages, the weakest. However, in Baodi County, some of the relatively better off villages have stronger Catholic atmospheres than do the poorer villages. To understand the connection between relative poverty and a strong Catholic atmosphere, we must understand the interplay between rural economic, political, and social structure.

The decisive factor in creating a strong or weak Catholic atmosphere seems to be whether the various interlocking institutions that constitute a rural community are open or closed. There are three dimensions to this factor, all relevant to the intensity of the Catholic atmosphere. Communities can be socially open or closed depending on how easy it is for members to move away. They can be economically open or closed depending on how much they are involved in regional or national markets. They can be politically open or closed depending on how closely their leaders are connected with the government or the Party. In the present context, different dimensions of an open or closed character lead to different degrees of economic development, which is why a Catholic atmosphere seems to be connected with wealth and poverty.

The rural communities with the strongest Catholic atmosphere tend to be the closed communities—closed along all three of the dimensions that I have distinguished. Compared with Xian County, Baodi is socially open. It has a surprisingly large number of university students for a rural area. In the village we studied most closely, in the previous four years four students had gone to a university (not necessarily the most prestigious universities, but teachers' colleges and technical schools) and had been able to establish residency in the city of Tianjin or in the county seat. Each of these students had given up the practice of Catholicism. "I didn't have time to pray because I was too busy with my studies," said one. "You have to follow the currents of society," said another. Because of the small but steady stream of Baodi residents who have been able to leave the countryside and gain an official urban residency, many Baodi villagers have family members in the city. The residency of family members in a city gives village families not only practical help, for instance in arranging business deals, but it also increases their social status, which makes them value somewhat the more secular, cosmopolitan atmosphere of the city.

However, because of the low quality of Xian County's schools, no one from there since the mid-1980s had passed the exams to go to a university. We met several young men who had failed the exams and had then decided that they had a vocation to the priesthood and had entered the seminary. Because the Chinese educational system offers the people of Xian County little hope of moving beyond their villages, they tend to disparage the content of that education, which in turn makes it even less likely that they will be able to use education as an avenue to secular upward mobility.

Some residents of Xian County live in Beijing, Tianjin, Shijiazhuang, and other cities, but either they went there in the 1950s, when it was easier for rural residents to move to the cities, or they have recently gone there illegally, as part of the "floating population."[26] In any case they have not gotten to the city by passing through official, secular channels; and they rely on their fellow Catholics from Xian County for help in getting along in the urban environment. Thus, they are relatively immune to those "currents of society" that push one to give up religious practice in order to get ahead.

It is, not surprisingly, in Xian County that one hears most of the talk about living in the world of God and the strongest affirmations that this world is incompatible with the modern world of science and commerce. Although, if asked, Catholic villagers in Baodi would say that the human world is sinful and corrupt, they tend to be quiet about their objections to it. By their deeds, many of them show their interest in getting involved in it.

Xian County's lack of economic opportunities is made more severe by its lack of political connections. For those in Xian County who saw themselves belonging to the world of God, the legacy of the Mao years was isolation from the world of politics. Although it depended on the amount of persecution they or their communities had directly suffered, the Xian County Catholics with whom we spoke were not necessarily hostile to politics. They decried the abuses of the Cultural Revolution, but they insisted that their faith made them good citizens. (If we had talked to members of the underground Church, we might have heard a different story.) "True believers," said a recently ordained priest, "abide by the rules of the Church, just as good citizens abide by the laws. . . . The Ten Commandments are more elaborate than the laws of the country—so a good believer is a good citizen. A good believer won't break the laws of the country." According to a young woman who aspires to be a nun, "Catholics abide by the law; they respect the laws even more than non-Catholics because the world of God includes the laws. If Catholics live in the world of God, they will be good citizens."

Although not hostile to politics, Catholics in Xian County receive little benefit from it. Since true-believing Catholics cannot be members of the Communist Party, they lack the political connections that make prosperity and upward mobility possible. Their attitude toward the Party seems to be one of ironic detachment. As a sixty-year-old man whose daughter is studying to be a nun said, "Party members get a lot of education, but not everybody does good things. Party members should be the first to suffer, the last to enjoy. But most of them are corrupt." While agreeing that "an individual who stands against the Party will come to a bad end," most Catholics in Xian County see no real benefit in standing closely with the Party. They place their hope in governing each other in their own communities according to the law of God. Often, their most important local leader is the local lay leader.

To a much fuller degree, Baodi villages are blended politically, as well as socially and economically, with the larger world. Not only did greater numbers of village families send their children on to higher education, but greater numbers worked in township industries and were involved in commerce. Some commuted regularly to the city of Tianjin. A number of village Catholics had joined the Communist Party, although their parents sometimes were horrified. "When I announced that I had joined the Party, my mother felt that she had lost face. . . . She begged me to return to the Church." Those who have joined the Party remain connected with their families, and, whatever the feelings of anguish parents have in regard to their wayward children, the family as a whole benefits from the connection to the power structure achieved by the Communist offspring. Sometimes, the parents who become upset with children who join the Party are precisely those who have taught their children to be ambitious, to seek connections with the wider world.

Social openness, then, erodes the faith and undermines the kind of social solidarity that would find its true home in a Church-dominated world of God. But to the extent that Chinese Catholic faith and community solidarity depend on being socially closed, the Catholic variety of social capital is ill-equipped to make a strong contribution to a civil society. Civil society is based on forms of community solidarity that encourage disciplined cooperation with rather than isolation from an open society.

Sociological factors—having a quasi-ethnic identity and being so-cially closed—have helped Catholic communities survive persecution. It may require theological innovation and moral conversion to enable such communities to play a constructive role in building a modern, plu-ralistic, civil society. Catholic agencies outside China have been making an effort to facilitate such theological innovation by supplying the Chi-nese Church—especially its seminaries—with teaching materials on the theology of the second Vatican Council, a theology that encour-ages relatively open communication between Catholics and the modern world.[27] But, to have an impact, such theological innovation would have to take place at higher levels than the local village community and would have to be disseminated through the networks that bind various local communities together. Even when local communities might be dis-posed to cooperate positively with non-Christian society, political pres-sures keep the larger Catholic community closed and alienated from Chinese society.

Many complicated ties do connect village-level Catholic communi-ties throughout China with one another and with the universal Catho-lic Church. First, local communities all share a common, distinctive time framework. They celebrate their festivals according to a common liturgical calendar. Second, they share a common religious vocabulary. These cultural commonalities are then circulated through a variety of communication links. Thus, even when Catholics are extremely invested in the life of their local village, they have both the motivation and the means to be in communication with other Catholic communities. For one thing, they will want if possible to marry their children to other Catholics. Such marriages usually entail links to Catholics beyond the confines of a village. Moreover, Catholics will want the services of an ordained priest, who, given the scarcity of priests in China, will have to travel a wide circuit. The priests available in a given area might include official and underground priests. Some Catholic communities might to-tally reject all officially approved priests; but even when Catholics ac-cept an officially approved priest, they may seek out an underground priest in time of crisis—for instance, when a family member is dying—because they may be more confident in the spiritual efficacy of the un-derground priest. The priests, both aboveground and underground, are in communication with the other priests in their diocese and often with networks of priests that extend well beyond diocesan boundaries.

Through all such connections, a great deal of news travels among lo-cal Catholic communities. Some of it is in the form of printed commu-

nication from officially approved clerical authorities: for instance, there
is a national Catholic magazine, as well as local newspapers for most
dioceses. But there are unofficial publications as well, like mimeographed leaflets that I have seen arguing the case for a particular underground bishop or reporting alleged apparitions of the Virgin Mary. Even
more important is word of mouth, which is how thousands in the Baoding diocese were called to brave police blockades and attend the funeral of the martyred Bishop Fan Xueyan in 1992. Foreigners facilitate
communication with the Chinese Church through radio broadcasts, including Vatican Radio, Radio Veritas (run by the Jesuits and transmitted from the Philippines), and SVD (Society of the Divine Word) Radio
(transmitted from Guam). Finally, news of the Church throughout
China and in the rest of world is carried by foreign visitors, often Chinese priests and religious from Taiwan and Hong Kong who make visits to the mainland, ostensibly to visit relatives.

Catholics seem eager to maintain such networks of communication,
which make them feel part of a larger world transcending their villages.
The problem with most of these networks, though, is that they are illegal. Their activation thus requires a web of personal trust, and the
act of carrying out surreptitious communication deepens the loyalties
among Catholic communication partners while at the same time helping to alienate them from the non-Catholic state and society. Often,
too, the nature of this forbidden communication helps to foment further division within the Church. While bringing many far-flung Catholics into contact, such communication is inevitably prone to distortion.
Rumor easily becomes hurtful gossip, which then breaks the Church
into factions. The modes of informal communication on which Catholics have to rely to come together thus increase their suspicion of outsiders and sow the seeds of dissension among themselves.

The potential for dissension is further increased by the circulation of
illicit money, as well as ideas, through these channels of communication. Besides bringing outside news, foreign visitors often bring money
to rebuild churches, carry out training programs and charitable works,
and supplement the meager incomes of priests and nuns. Contributed
by Catholic missionary societies, Catholic dioceses, and Catholic advocacy organizations throughout the world, some of this money is for the
underground Church, some for the official Church. But even much of
the foreign money given to the official Church is illegal in the eyes of the
Chinese government. The money that comes from foreigners, moreover,
often comes with partisan messages. For instance, money earmarked for

the underground Church sometimes comes from agencies, like the Cardinal Kung Foundation, that want the underground to be as uncompromising as possible.[28] Although necessary to help the Chinese Catholic Church meet its material needs, outside money usually needs to be hidden from non-Catholics and is the cause of mutual jealousy among Catholics. Thus, it often strengthens the viruses of suspicion infecting the trustful solidarity of the Catholic community.

Even as it moves to isolate itself from what it sees as a godless environment, the world of God in China thus takes on some of the vices of that environment—truculence, paranoia, contentiousness. Catholic solidarity is no better than most forms of solidarity that are shaped by the pressures of a corrupt and oppressive regime. To contribute to a viable civil society, the Catholic community would have to constantly seek to become better than its society—more magnanimous, more trusting, more cooperative. In principle, the Christian message provides spiritual resources for developing such qualities of character. In the next chapter we shall explore in what ways the Chinese Church does or does not sustain them in practice.

CHAPTER THREE

Morality and Spirituality

Whether they believe deeply or not, China's rural Catholics find themselves part of clearly identified communities, the particular history and social circumstances of which produce varying levels of both social solidarity and hostility toward outsiders. From this point of view, Catholicism exerts its influence on individuals from the outside. But, to varying degrees, many Catholics take the faith to heart. Thus internalized, it influences their moral character and their sense of the meaning and purpose of life. Although each person internalizes the faith in a particular way, true-believing Catholics tend to display a characteristic morality—that is, a disposition to particular patterns of virtue and vice—and a characteristic spirituality—that is, a style of thinking and feeling about the meaning of their lives and the nature of their relationship with God and with the world.[1] How does their morality influence the ways they cooperate and conflict with one another and with non-Catholics? How does their spirituality guide their response to the challenges posed by social change in China?

MORALITY AND CHARACTER

Although rural Catholics believe that it is virtually impossible to eradicate a Catholic identity, that even an extremely indifferent Catholic is still a Catholic, they also assume that some Catholics are better than others. A relentless flux of gossip pressures even the lax to reach toward the standards of local moral exemplars. Village gossip consists of un-remitting talk, laced with moral judgments, about the behavior of personal acquaintances. It is a particular style of speech, nicely illustrated by the following words from one of our interviewees, a middle-aged true-believing woman: "There is a person," she says in a bossy voice, "who, after praying, did bad things; so people criticized him, said, 'Look at him doing such things just after leaving the church!' I felt ashamed of him. If I were him, I would never go to church, not even to kneel!"

In Catholic villages, the church becomes one of the most important focal points of local gossip networks. Those who go to church and fail to live up to the moral demands of village Catholicism face vigorous backbiting. The gossip is often contentious. Perhaps the most frequently violated moral code of Catholic villagers is the one that says that villagers should not quarrel with one another. Paradoxically, the quarreling is often connected with the gossip that is so instrumental in creating and enforcing local moral standards.

These standards demand that morality be a matter of character, not simply of formal religious practice. As a seventy-year-old Catholic woman says, "There are some fervent Catholics who go to the Church every day and do so much kneeling that their knees are sore; but if they don't abide by the laws of the Church, it's no good." Faith is worthless without good works; and, in the end, good works are worthless without good intentions, without the purity of a good heart.

These standards are consistent not only with the Thomistic philosophy that was the basis of the nineteenth-century missionaries' catechism but also with classical Confucian philosophy. According to both of these "great traditions," morality involves an interplay between rules and character. In the Chinese formulation, morality is both *lunli*—the norms that regulate how persons should perform their social roles—and *daode*—the virtues (*de*) that one must cultivate in order to reach the ineffable, transcendent, ultimate meaning of things (*dao*). To be a moral person, one must know and abide by the myriad rules governing social relations. But one needs virtue—an internalized set of habits—to follow the rules faithfully, to give a consistent structure and stability to one's intentions, to reconcile competing responsibilities, and to act properly when the rules are ambiguous. Only by being a person of virtue can one achieve the purpose of the moral life, which is to be one with the *dao*, the ultimate meaning of things—or, in Catholic teaching, to gain salvation.

For Chinese Catholics, the rules for moral life are the Ten Commandments. True-believing Catholics are proud to be able to recite these commands by heart. But although they see the Ten Commandments as central to Catholic morality, they also widely assume that these Biblical rules are essentially the same as the rules accepted by all decent people, non-Catholics as well as Catholics. "What's important in life," said a thirty-year-old Catholic mother of two, "is to be a good person—no stealing, no defrauding." The phrase she used (*bu tou, bu mo*) is a conventional Chinese idiom for the essence of good morality. "Whatever religion you belong to," she believes, "says that you are not supposed to abuse or cheat [*bu keng ren, bu pian ren*]." To these commandments, most villagers add: "do not gamble, drink to excess, commit adultery, or curse."

It is not only that Chinese Catholic moral codes are virtually the same as non-Catholic ones but also by Catholics' own admission, that Catholic moral practice is generally the same as non-Catholic, no better, no worse. Some Catholics say that Catholics should be better than non-Catholics; but they usually admit that this is not the case. Some non-Catholic villagers say that Catholics are less moral than non-Catholics—they let their goats graze in non-Catholic fields; they curse and argue and engage in petty theft. But most non-Catholics with whom we spoke admitted that some non-Catholics do such things too and that Catholics really were not much worse than anybody else. This commonality of moral norms and practice gives individual Catholics a reason to transcend their community boundaries and enter into relations of mutual respect with non-Catholic individuals. In the end, what is important is not whether you are a Catholic but what kind of person you are, what virtues you have.

But what is a good person? Most Catholics may tacitly agree on the basic norms of right and wrong. But all individuals, at least some of the time, fall short of these norms. How do you tell whose sins are forgivable? How do you tell who should, in spite of their faults, be admired as exemplars of virtue? Who, in short, has a good moral character?

LOYALTY AS THE CARDINAL VIRTUE

Although Catholic villagers see norms of morality as the same everywhere (they do not have a clear idea about how different the norms are in other cultures), when they make judgments about character they pay close attention to how the norms have been applied in particular social contexts and to how well, in following the norms, individual people throughout life have served their home community. A good person is someone who has been good for a Catholic community. In practice, loyalty seems to be the cardinal virtue.[2] People of poor character are those who are consistently disloyal, who consistently use others for their own selfish ends. If they treat their neighbors in this way, some Catholics say, they will treat God the same way. Thus a village woman criticized one of her neighbors for constantly using other people, and she commented that the woman had a utilitarian attitude toward God as well: "when she needs help, she goes to Church, but after her problem has passed, she forgets God."

Reflecting the pervasive Chinese folk culture, the gossips who enunciate the informal moral standards in villages generally assume that the worst kinds of people are those who are disloyal, or "unfilial," to their parents. In one village we visited there was much criticism of a young man who had been raised by a widowed mother. The mother had refused to remarry because "it wouldn't have been good for her son to have a stepfather." Over the years, the woman saved to build a new house so that when it came time for her son to marry, he could attract a good bride. Eventually a match was made with an energetic, attractive young woman who had once contemplated becoming a nun. But after the son married, his wife said that she did not want to share her house with her mother-in-law. The old woman was forced to move back into the run-down building that had been her original house. Because she could not count on her child and his wife to take care of her in her old age, she decided to marry an old widower. She did not want to remarry, but she had no choice given the way her son, influenced by his wife, treated her. Many villagers therefore had a low opinion of her son and his wife. They thought that the couple demonstrated the worst kind of character defect, unfilialness.

For all the talk about the Ten Commandments, then, the rural Catholic moral imagination is dominated by the Fourth Commandment—honor thy father and mother—and by the virtue of family loyalty, which makes adherence to that commandment reliable and consistent.[3] Loyalty toward parents is both the core of good character and the core of a right relation to God. As a thirty-year-old Catholic mother says, "Belief in God is just like having filial piety toward parents. A person cannot forget his parents, should speak with them often, should not be indifferent to them."

Loyalty to family is complemented by loyalty to local community, especially to the local Catholic community. People who happen to do the right thing simply because it is in their self-interest cannot be truly good people. However, people who do the right thing not necessarily because it is intrinsically good but because it is in the interest of their local community are good people. Indeed, one important reason for doing good, says a leader of a Catholic village in Xian County, is to maintain the reputation of the community. "People who can't follow the Catholic law are mocked by non-Catholics. The non-Catholics, of course, won't say these things openly. They will gossip secretly."

Since loyalty to family and community is the primary virtue, someone whom most Catholics in a given community think of as having a good character may not be judged in the same way by outsiders, especially non-Catholics. Insofar as good character is judged in terms of what helps the local Catholic community, sins against non-Catholics are not quite as bad as those against Catholics. The universalistic morality of the Ten Commandments gets refracted through the particularistic morality of the familistic culture of rural life.

Non-Catholics are thus irritated that Catholics allegedly do not fully respect non-Catholics' property. Catholics say that it is wrong to steal from anyone, but they tend to gloss over infringements on the property of non-Catholics, especially if they benefit the Catholic community. For example, a respected Catholic village leader told about a big tree that was standing on the spot where the Catholics wanted to build a church. The tree belonged to non-Catholics, who did not want it cut down. "But, miraculously, one night the tree was removed." The Catholic leader obviously did not want to place any weight on the transgression that lay behind the miracle. Rural non-Catholics judge character in a similar relativistic way. Members of a particular community overlook the faults of those who are loyal to them; outsiders do not overlook those faults, especially if they have suffered as a result of them.

LOYALTY AS A CENTRAL VICE

When overemphasized, most virtues tend to turn into mirror-image vices. The virtue of loyalty becomes the vice of a rigid particularism, a narrowness of heart that sacrifices the greater good for the sake of one's small community. The rural Catholic moral style is often afflicted with this vice. Take, for instance, the case of Chen Liyan, a proud, handsome woman, now in her fifties, from a traditionally Catholic family. When she was young, she was good-looking and a beautiful singer. During the

Cultural Revolution she met her husband—a non-Catholic—while they both were working in an amateur drama troupe. When her future husband wanted to marry her, she said that she must remain loyal to the faith of her family; she would never marry him unless he converted to Catholicism. The young man's family was having a hard time making a good match for their son, so they finally agreed to her condition. Perhaps, at the time, it did not seem extremely important. "It was during the Cultural Revolution when we got married," she recalled. "Nobody [outside of Catholic communities like hers] cared about religion then."

However, in the early 1990s, she sounded positively triumphant as she described how she had pressured her husband to convert. The triumphalism seemed to betray an un-Christian satisfaction with dominating people. Forcing her husband to convert to Catholicism was a first step in winning a power struggle with her in-laws. When her father-in-law died, she would not allow her husband to perform the customary folk-religious rituals for his father. So the whole village—both Catholics and non-Catholics—laughed at him, thinking him really pitiable.

Now she treats her bedridden mother-in-law badly. When asked about her relationship with her mother-in-law, she says, "We have nothing to say to each other. My duty is to give her three meals a day. She was not happy that my husband was baptized, but that is none of her business. The grandchildren were baptized, and she was unhappy about that too, but she couldn't do anything about it." The mother-in-law sleeps in a messy room on an exceptionally dirty kang. On the dark walls of the mother-in-law's room are several pictures of the Virgin Mary. When asked whether her mother-in-law feels happy about having such pictures over her bed, Chen Liyan simply says, "This is *my* house." When asked why her mother-in-law let her son marry a Catholic, Chen Liyan says, "That was her mistake." For the old mother-in-law, this must be the worst nightmare about a mixed marriage come true. In this Catholic woman's way of interpreting the Fourth Commandment, the virtue of loyalty thus gets turned into a vice of familistic selfishness. This is a common vice of rural non-Catholics as well as of Catholics. In its pattern of virtues and vices, Catholic morality takes on the coloration of ordinary Chinese rural folk morality.

An important consequence of this loyalty-centered morality is factionalism. Catholics believe that they should bestow the highest degrees of honor on those who have displayed heroic degrees of loyalty and that they should bestow such honor by elevating such heroes to positions of community leadership. Since heroic loyalty often comes perilously close to vice, however, Catholic communities may fall under the sway of rigid absolutists rather than flexible conciliators.

In judging character, Catholic villagers do not expect that ordinary people can be absolutely loyal under all circumstances. They expect their fellow Catholics to maintain their loyalty under normal circumstances, when they are not under an unreasonable amount of pressure. What constitutes an unreasonable amount of pressure is a matter for debate, part of an ongoing conversation about what Catholic morality really means in the messy circumstances of life. Consider, for example, Catholic villagers' judgments of people who renounced their faith under political pressure during the Cultural Revolution. An eighty-year-old woman from Xian County says, "During the Cultural Revolution, everybody was asked to renounce their faith, but nobody really renounced it. Maybe some people renounced it orally. But I don't think they betrayed God in their hearts."

There is therefore a basis for reconciliation between Catholics who took more and less heroic stands in defense of their faith during the Cultural Revolution. When churches were rebuilt and reopened after the mid-1980s, they were filled with crowds of enthusiastic worshipers; in many cases virtually the entire Catholic population of villages, the lax and the devout, saints and sinners alike, came together. Those who had failed to be courageous witnesses to the faith during the Cultural Revolution were not necessarily excluded. In the villages that we visited, we did not discern any outward signs of animosity toward lay Catholics who had failed to stand up for their beliefs during the Cultural Revolution. However, such people are not moral exemplars, deserving of special honor and respect. Some Catholics underwent torture rather than renounce their faith, and Catholics believe that they deserve a special kind of admiration and loyalty. Disagreement arises over what form this admiration and loyalty should take. We met a man, for instance, who was singled out by Red Guards because he had been a lay leader in his village. They dragged him out on a stage for a "struggle session," and they demanded that he renounce his faith. He refused. They beat him and made him crawl on his knees until the knee bones were exposed. They locked him in a "cowshed" (local prison) and labeled him a "black hand." After he was released, he was ostracized within the community. He did not dare speak to anyone. No one dared to publicly associate with him. Now that Cultural Revolution stigmas have been removed, he is once again an active leader. But he seems to be working independently of the official Church. He has built a chapel inside his house. This "house church" is filled with worshipers on Sundays, even though a handsome, officially opened Church is only about a ten-minute walk away (but in a different village). Because of his martyrdom, he is widely admired. Even Catholics who are almost completely indifferent spoke about him with great respect. However, everyone does not want to worship in his chapel. The official church is widely attended as well. Although Catholics may continue to revere the Cultural Revolution martyr, they do not necessarily want to get into political trouble now any more than they did during the Cultural Revolution, when they refused to stick their necks out in defense of the faith.

I found a similar attitude in the city when I asked Catholics connected with the officially opened Tianjin cathedral what they thought of Bishop Li Side, the leader of the diocese's underground Church. Although they did not think that Bishop Li was right to denounce Catholics in the official Church and did not think that his course of adamant resistance was wise under the circumstances, they expressed great respect for him. He is a good man, they said. He has suffered greatly for the Church and is a good example for the faith. It was as if they believed that the loyalty of Church martyrs deserved to be repaid at least with moral loyalty, though not necessarily with practical affiliation. But many others claim that loyalty to Bishop Li and to other local martyrs must be expressed through staunch commitment to their leadership. Given the centrality of the virtue of loyalty in the moral imagination of Chinese Catholics, those who are uncompromisingly loyal to fellow Catholics who have loyally suffered martyrdom can claim a preeminent moral superiority.

Similar to other underground bishops and priests, Bishop Li lays great stress on how much he has suffered for the faith and how, because of that suffering, he and his followers cannot compromise with the government. But this emphasis on uncompromising, martyred loyalty sometimes fosters a rigid intransigence. The leader who bases his legitimacy on such heroic loyalty to the faith cannot afford to compromise, even when compromise might be called for by Christ's commands to "judge not, lest you be judged" and to "love your enemies, do good to those who hate you." Given the centrality of loyalty in the Sinified Catholic moral imagination, Catholics who most aspire to overcome their weaknesses and atone for their sins tend to form self-righteous, unforgiving factions centered around leaders who have made a strong claim to martyrdom.

The government obliges this spirit of intransigent self-righteousness by continuing to produce martyrs. It intensified persecution of the underground Church from 1989 until 1993. Then, for a brief period, probably in order to improve its human-rights record in the hope of being chosen to host the Olympics in 2000, it released many underground Catholic clergy (along with secular dissidents like Wei Jingsheng) from prison. But by 1994 the repression had intensified, and it continues to the present day. In lists published by Amnesty International and Human Rights Watch/Asia, the number of Catholics in prison for practicing their faith is comparable to the number of secular dissidents in prison for attempting to promote democracy.[4]

Given the centrality of loyalty to Chinese Catholics, the repression simply deepens the intransigence of those most strongly committed. And while it may intimidate some, it mobilizes others who may have been prone to compromise and reconciliation. Even those who do not think that heroic loyalty in the face of persecution necessarily qualifies a Catholic to be an authoritative leader believe that such loyalty deserves honor and respect. But even this belief contradicts the propaganda of the government, which claims that Catholic martyrs are not religious loyalists but political subversives, not persons of exemplary character but traitors to the state. Interfering with the traditional Church calendar, the Chinese Catholic Patriotic Association has gone so far as to eliminate all feasts of the martyrs from the liturgical year. (Yet it organized prayer meetings after June 4, 1989, "in thanksgiving for the government's victory over the rebels in Tiananmen Square.")[5] Under these circumstances, when the government creates new Catholic martyrs, it can easily provoke a widespread negative reaction from all Catholics, not only those closely connected to the underground Church. Such was the case with the demonstrations at the funeral of Bishop Fan Xueyan, after Catholics heard rumors that he had been tortured to death in prison. Bishop Fan had been a divisive force in the Chinese Catholic Church. He had issued a document in 1988 saying that Catholics who participate in worship in the official churches commit a mortal sin.[6] But even those who continued to participate in the official Church may have been united with underground Catholics in their repugnance toward the government's treatment of Bishop Fan and in their need as a community to affirm that he was a good man, not a disloyal citizen, as the government wanted him labeled.

The government's repression serves to polarize and factionalize Catholic communities and in the process to inflame the vice of intransigence that is a close companion of the virtue of loyalty. This result is probably what the government wants; it is following a divide-and-conquer strategy. But if the government ever should collapse, the task of rebuilding a new China will be made difficult because Catholic communities (as well as other religious communities) are riddled with the vices that cause division rather than blessed with the virtues that bring peace.

SPIRITUALITY AND THE RESOLUTION OF MORAL DILEMMAS

Yet the Chinese Catholic Church is not without resources to transcend its folk-cultural vices. It is true that the moral judgments rendered by village gossip tend to be apodictic—not usually qualified or contingent, not distinguishing shades of gray. But, while individually unambiguous, the moral judgments rendered in gossip may collectively be quite subtle. Taken in the aggregate, they often draw a picture consisting of many sharp dots of black and white that sometimes contradict one another, so when you bring together all the judgments that gossips render about someone, you do get half-tones, shades of gray.

Because inner moral intention is so important, says the lay leader of a Xian County Catholic village, "it is difficult to distinguish between lax and true-believing Catholics because someone who goes to Church regularly may not believe in God truly." Despite their delight in judging one another's behavior negatively, rural Catholics themselves recognize—albeit somewhat abstractly—that one cannot ever know for sure who is a good and who is a bad Catholic, who is a saint and who is a sinner. Goodness and evil lie buried in the heart.

Catholic villagers know, too, that real goodness involves magnanimity and generosity as well as loyalty. "A good Catholic," says a middle-aged mother, "should bear with other people and be willing to suffer a loss rather than taking advantage of anybody else. The reason people believe in Jesus is that he had this spirit of sacrifice for others. This came from deep within himself. Jesus had twelve disciples, and one of them betrayed him—and Jesus still was willing to wash his feet [at the Last Supper]." Being a good Catholic, according to a seventy-year-old woman who was raised in a Catholic orphanage, is a matter of following the Sermon on the Mount. "Pious Catholics should learn to do good. Love God above, love people here on earth. Don't do anything against another person's will. Seek and you will find, knock and it will be opened. . . . Love everyone as you love yourself." Even the report from Beijing University is impressed with—although worried about some of the effects of—the love and generosity prevalent in some Catholic communities. It cites the case of a Communist Party cadre who, on becoming seriously ill, was ignored by his fellow Party members but warmly helped by local Catholics. As a result he gave up his Party membership and joined the Church.[7]

In the end, devout Catholics believe, doing good is not merely a matter of winning approval from the gossips or general respect from community members; it is a matter of eternal salvation or damnation. As rural Chinese Catholics talk about it, salvation is decidedly other-worldly—a matter of going to heaven and avoiding hell. They talk a great deal—more than most Catholics in the West—about heaven and hell. As a thirty-five-year-old Catholic man puts it, "Life is short, but heaven is forever." After death, they say confidently, those who have been baptized, have prayed regularly, and have received the sacraments will go to heaven, usually after a stint in the fires of purgatory. Bad people will go to hell. Good people who have not been baptized will go to limbo. Chinese Catholics are concerned about how, in spite of the confusions and disappointments they have all experienced, they might get to heaven. Such concern about Last Things impels many of them to think seriously and creatively about the meaning of their lives. It gives them a complex, dynamic spirituality that can provide subtle answers to the moral dilemmas they face because of China's changing economic and political circumstances.

Take, for example, their use of the doctrine of limbo. The notion of limbo was never clearly developed by the medieval Catholic Church, and it is now virtually forgotten by most Catholics in the West, but it was an important part of the theology brought to China in the late nineteenth and early twentieth centuries by foreign missionaries. Some of those rural Catholics whom we interviewed now use this doctrine creatively to understand their place in a pluralistic society. Their forebears were taught that there was no salvation outside the Church—that, as Pope Benedict XV put it in his 1919 encyclical *Maximum Illud,* the purpose of missionary work was to save "the numberless heathen still sitting in the shadows of death."[8] The theology of the second Vatican Council reinterpreted the old doctrine that "outside the Church there is no salvation" to mean that the grace of salvation, though given through the Church, was available to everyone of good will in the world, even those belonging to different religions who never entered the Church. Vatican II's theology thus encouraged Catholics to have an attitude of respect toward and solidarity with non-Catholics and even toward non-Christians.

Without access to the teachings of Vatican II, Chinese Catholics nonetheless made use of the doctrine of limbo to sustain a positive attitude toward their non-Catholic acquaintances. Although non-Catholics will not go to heaven, they say, the non-Catholics will not necessarily be claimed by the devil. They will go to limbo, which is not all that bad a place. Some of the Chinese Catholics with whom we spoke filled the empty doctrine of limbo with a rich Chinese folk-religious content. A thirty-year-old woman married to a non-Catholic told us she sometimes gives a priest money to say a Black Mass (a Mass for the dead) for her deceased, non-Christian mother-in-law. She is not sure what good this will do, but she thinks it may have the same effect as the non-Catholic practice of burning mock paper money at funerals. The non-Catholic funeral practice is supposed to provide spending money for the deceased in the netherworld. Perhaps the real money given to the priest for the Black Mass will somehow end up in the hands of her mother-in-law in the other world. Limbo then becomes the same as the ordinary folk-religious conception of a world after death—a place where one's ancestors live pretty much as they do in this world, with the aid of money and food sent to them via sacrificial offerings. In this view, non-Catholics will receive no surprises after death other than not finding their Catholic neighbors around because the Catholics, at least the good ones, will have gone to a much better place.

MARY, MIRACLES, AND THE INSTITUTIONAL CHURCH

Besides finding home-grown theological rationales for civil cooperation with non-Catholic neighbors, Catholic villagers can also find their own spiritual reasons to get around the factional pressures that afflict the Church hierarchy. The institutional Church, as they experience it, is a cold, somewhat harsh, authoritarian structure, confusing because of its internal divisions. It is presided over by a harsh deity. God, as most Catholic villagers imagine him, is a stern accountant. A fifty-year-old woman describes what God will do to a sinner kneeling to face him. "God will never help him because he is full of sin. God knows his sins. God will note this in his account book. Such a person will not come to a good end after death." A Chinese Catholic seminarian now living in the United States finds it odd that American Catholics speak of Jesus as a "friend." "We think of Jesus not as a friend, but as a ruler." [9]

Nevertheless, Chinese Catholics still find a warm and compassionate dimension of the sacred in the Virgin Mary. The central pictures in most rural churches and most true-believing Catholic homes are of the Blessed Virgin. According to many of those with whom we spoke, the primary focus of belief is not God the Father but Mary, "who is our mother." The Marian cult was central to the theology conveyed to China by nineteenth- and twentieth-century European missionaries. Mary—gentle, compassionate Mary, portrayed even in Chinese households as a slender, brown-haired European woman dressed in blue, often openly displaying her Immaculate Heart—is primarily the one who helps us in our trials, defends us from our enemies, heals us when we are sick, and keeps us from sin. The eager acceptance of the Marian cult by Chinese Catholics was the result at least partly of Mary's similarity to the Buddhist Guanyin and to the Eternal Mother of north Chinese secret societies.

Through the Marian cult Chinese Catholics can solve some of the spiritual dilemmas presented by conflicts within the Church. Chinese Catholics were raised on a catechesis that stressed the importance of receiving the sacraments for achieving salvation. But during the Cultural Revolution, when people were enduring the most terrible sufferings and being forced to confront the most horrible evils, almost no priests were available. Did their inability to receive the sacraments at this time mean that after living in a hell on earth, most Catholics could have no hope of heaven in the next life? Even now there is a great shortage of priests, and those who are available are split into official and underground factions, which sometimes claim that it is a mortal sin to receive sacraments from a priest on the other side.

Chinese Catholics were taught by their missionaries that in cases of necessity they could baptize their children themselves and thus bring their children within the salvific bosom of the Church. As noted in the previous chapter, most children born to true-believing Catholic families were thus secretly baptized, usually by their mothers or grandmothers. If an infant dies after receiving this home baptism, Catholics believe the child will go not to limbo but to heaven. Although official Catholic theology would say that the home baptism (provided that it is administered properly and the right words are said) is a perfectly valid baptism and makes one fully a member of the Catholic Church, in the thinking of most ordinary rural Catholics the home baptism does not count as much as a baptism performed by a priest inside a church. As they see it, the "provisional baptism" (*daixi*) needs to be brought to completion through a formal baptism (*lingxi*), administered with all the proper cer-

Figure 8. Altar of a rural church; note the centrality of the Marian image.
Photograph by Richard Madsen.

emonies. They seem to suspect that a person, especially an adult, who
has never received a formal baptism cannot enter heaven.

True-believing Catholics are thus eager to have a priest administer
baptism. But suppose the only priest around is one who is affiliated with
the Chinese Catholic Patriotic Association, and suppose one believes
that to affiliate with that Association is to betray the Church? Should
one receive the sacrament anyway, from such a bad priest? Some Catholics believe so strongly that God's saving grace comes only through the
institutional Church that they may be willing to receive baptism and
the other sacraments from a priest who they think has failed in his commitment to the Vatican. But in recent years some of the leaders of the
underground Church have been saying that anyone who receives the
sacraments from a priest in the official Church is thereby excommunicated—expelled from the Church and thus without hope of salvation.

So true-believing Catholics worry excruciatingly about related theological questions. How badly does one need a formal baptism, with all the ceremonies? How necessary is it to receive Holy Communion regularly? If one has sinned, how essential is it to have one's sins absolved by a priest in the sacrament of penance? How important is it to have one's marriage blessed by a priest? What will happen if one dies without having received the sacrament of extreme unction? When a priest administers the sacraments, is grace bestowed automatically, *ex opere operato,* no matter whether the priest is a good or bad man, or does saving grace depend on the goodness of the minister? Is it more important to receive the sacraments than to face the threat of excommunication? Just how valid is the excommunication proclaimed by embittered underground priests?

Devotion to Mary helps to alleviate some of these worries. Holy Mother Mary is warm and full of mercy. She is like one's own mother— the mother who, in her own bedroom, quietly poured the first waters of baptism on one's head, the mother who provides perhaps the only glimpses of warmth and caring one will ever experience in the world. Mary thus can bring salvation directly, outside the institutional structures of the Church. The more deeply one believes in this avenue of salvation, the less one's salvation is held hostage to the rivalries between the men of the official Church and the underground Church and to the political machinations of the powerful Religious Affairs Bureau.

Although, remembering their catechisms, true-believing Catholics say that the sacraments, properly administered by a priest, are the primary channels of grace, they in practice rely on Mary to give them a chance at heaven. One colloquial name for Catholics in the north China countryside is "Old Rosary Sayers." Certainly, they spend much more time saying the rosary to Mary than going to Mass. The most pious Catholics meet every day for morning and evening recitation of the rosary (a ritual that bears a striking similarity to popular Buddhist practices). As a Catholic woman from Xian County says, "Every morning people need to thank God for giving them a good night, for protecting their soul and body, . . . [to] ask God to protect them so that everything will pass in peace. Before going to bed, they need to pray again." Usually, these prayers take place in the village church and, where there is no church, in a believer's house. Although during the Cultural Revolution many Catholics were content to say the rosary privately, some still risked persecution by gathering in small groups to quietly mumble the familiar Our Fathers and Hail Marys.

Besides helping to save Catholics from the inadequacies of their ecclesiastical institution, Mary helps to defend them from the pressures of a hostile state and society. Apparitions of the Blessed Virgin play an important part in the spiritual imaginations of Chinese Catholics. The report from Beijing University mentions a mass movement, eventually crushed by the government, of many thousands of Shanxi Catholics in response to an apparition of Mary on a mountain near Taiyuan.[10] There are shrines to Marian apparitions throughout China. Some of these become major pilgrimage sites—for instance, the shrine at Sheshan, near Shanghai, and, in north China, at Donglu, near Baoding.

The shrine at Donglu, which was shut down and desecrated in 1996, is the one most central to the spirituality of the Catholics we visited in Hebei. Almost every village in this region has a story of how Holy Mary appeared in 1900, when the village was encircled by enemies during the Boxer rebellion, and drove away the Boxers. Apparently the most spectacular of these interventions occurred at Donglu. During the Cultural Revolution, a church in Donglu was torn down. In the early 1980s, when it again became possible to worship in public, some villagers put up a picture of the Virgin Mary in an open space where the church had stood, and as many as twenty thousand pilgrims came every year to worship in front of the picture. In the late 1980s, the six thousand Catholics of Donglu began to build a huge new church, a twin-spired, Gothic-style basilica that can hold several thousand worshipers. It is an enormously impressive accomplishment, a tribute to an extraordinary collective devotion.[11] In 1995 the *Washington Post* described a crowd of around ten thousand attending a Mass celebrated by an underground priest outside the Church. The people squinted into the midday sun hoping to catch their own glimpses of Mary.[12]

Some of them probably did. In his brilliant study of Marian apparitions in a small town in Germany, the historian David Blackbourne concludes that "modern European apparitions have occurred in clusters, usually at periods of particular stress. The triggers have most commonly been economic crisis, epidemic, war, and political persecution."[13] Apparitions in West Germany ceased once it attained stability and prosperity after the Second World War. China has continued to provide many of the triggers mentioned by Blackbourne, and we would expect that for pious Catholics China will continue to be a fertile site for apparitions.

Besides central pilgrimage sites like Donglu, many local shrines have been the sites of apparitions; the Hebei village of Fanjiagade, for example, prints a small mimeographed booklet promoting its local cult.

Figure 9. Marian basilica at Donglu, closed and desecrated by police forces in the fall of 1996. Photograph courtesy of Jean Charbonnier, *Guide to the Catholic Church in China*.

Figure 10. Painting of Our Lady of China venerated at Donglu; this painting has since been carried away by police forces. Photograph courtesy of Jean Charbonnier, *Guide to the Catholic Church in China.*

As has been the case with reports of Marian apparitions throughout the world in the past two centuries, Chinese Church leaders do not encourage people to believe in these apparitions and are prone to discourage cults surrounding a place of apparition. Church officials, like government officials, do not like popular mass movements they cannot control. But when a movement gets too popular for them to suppress, they try to co-opt it, as they are now in China. Supervised by the Religious Affairs Bureau, the top leaders of the Church approve some central places of Marian worship and discourage others. Still, Mary appears where she wants, bringing salvation to ordinary believers who cannot trust their weakened and politically compromised ecclesiastical institutions and who feel themselves threatened by uncontrollable political and economic forces. One might even predict that precisely because of the government's assaults on Donglu, Mary will be appearing there more often than ever.

In the end, perhaps, as Blackbourne says of the European apparitions he has studied, such events "can be seen as a form of revolt against modernity, against modern economic life and the modern state." [14] The Chinese Catholics' belief in Marian apparitions is closely connected with their general belief in miracles, a belief that defies all the education about science they receive in their schools. Catholics talk about miracles a lot. Almost all the true-believing Catholics we asked said they had personally experienced miracles, and they often claimed that their faith was strong precisely because they had been blessed with such experiences.

The most commonly cited miracles are humble acts of unexplained good fortune. A sixty-year-old man had his mule run away. "As usual when I meet difficulties, I prayed to God. . . . The mule ran for about a half mile and then stopped suddenly. When I came close, I found that there was a rope tied around the mule's legs. I looked around but found no one. Who did that? God helped me!" To his great consternation, a young man had the wind blow an important financial document out of his hand. Though he despaired of finding it, all of a sudden he saw it stuck in a bush. After that, he was converted from being a lukewarm Catholic to being a firm believer.

God grants these miracles, usually through the intercession of the Virgin Mary, without going through any priest or following any ecclesiastical rule. All that is necessary is that the individual believer sincerely seek God's help. The miracles are independent of any human effort. Sometimes, miracles are a way for God to give the believer a calling to serve the Church directly, without the believer's having to get the approval of any official authority.

Even though rural Catholics talk of salvation as concerning their afterlife, their talk about miracles brings salvation back into this world. As they often speak of them, miracles are God's way of making up for human mistakes. They help people who were careless in watching over their mule or in keeping their important papers safe. This belief in miracles helps to make sense of the messy, uncontrollable aspect of life in contemporary rural China. Much about that life defies rational planning: all too often in the Chinese countryside economic-development programs have had unforeseen, disastrous consequences; what appear to be the best laid plans go astray; things fall apart. Talk about miracles holds out the hope that in spite of the failure of human agents, people's lives will still work out all right. Through miracles, God and Mary help even those who do not help themselves.

Although these miraculous experiences are individual and idiosyncratic, they are deeply connected with family and community relations. Miracles usually make it possible to fulfill responsibilities toward family and community members. Miracles come to those who have lived a good life by community standards. A rural Chinese Catholic's miraculous salvation makes him or her a part of a particular kind of community, one centered on family life in an unpredictable, rural milieu: a still wild world, undominated by any carefully constituted Church hierarchy or tightly organized state structure, a place where people still feel at the mercy of random natural and social forces, where improvised coping rather than systematic planning is often the only way to get along.

It is a world connected with that of the Big Teaching, rural folk religion, as well as distinguished from it. Catholic and non-Catholic Chinese villagers attribute similar kinds of good luck and unusual experiences to the supernatural. Catholics attribute them to God, non-Catholics to ancestors or perhaps to Bodhisattvas. This world, however, is being displaced by a new world emanating from the cities: a world of market forces, entrepreneurial opportunities, rational calculation—in short, a modern world of economic development. Does the Catholic faith make it easier or more difficult to join this world?

ANTIMODERNISM

According to most of the rural true believers with whom we spoke, their faith puts them in principled opposition not simply to Communism but to modernity in general. Secular schooling is especially problematic for such devout Catholics. They complained about the "materialistic" nature of education in China and felt called to combat this godless education. Even more than to the Marxist political ideology that was taught in the schools they objected to the natural science. They were not necessarily against all expansion of human knowledge through study of the natural world, and several of them stressed that some of the great scientists, like Newton, believed in God. But they found some of the main scientific discoveries of the nineteenth and twentieth centuries incompatible with the Catholic faith. Several mentioned their objections to theories of evolution and to the idea that the universe originated in a "big bang." In the words of a thirty-three-year-old country priest, "The education our youth have received is materialistic and atheistic. . . . Do people come from monkeys? Never!" Several mentioned that they had read (in materials distributed to many Catholics) that Noah's ark had been found in the Himalayas, which they argued proved the Bible's literal account of early human history.

True belief also entails a rejection of the economic forces that have been driving China's development. From the point of view of devout village Catholics, the world of contemporary Chinese commerce seems like a cesspool of corruption and greed. Says the lay leader of one of the Catholic villages in Xian County, "I agree with what the bishop said [in his Christmas sermon on the previous day in 1993]: 'blessed are the poor.' The purpose of living in the world is not to seek enjoyment. . . . In my opinion, Catholic teaching is contrary to human desires. I'm not opposed to making money by working hard. But I feel confused about how to reconcile making money with obeying the teaching of God. I always teach my children not to be too greedy. It is very clear that social darkness is descending on this place—gambling, drinking, quarreling—because the world of God has lost its strength."

China's current rapid economic growth is the consequence of a no-holds-barred, free-wheeling market economy, heavily lubricated by graft. Those who are not driven to make a lot of money quickly and who are scrupulous about playing by the rules are simply not going to be in the forefront of the entrepreneurial revolution that is transforming the Chinese economy. A middle-aged Catholic widow who made a little money selling wheat cakes in the market told us that she did not cheat her customers because the cakes were all made the same size and the customers knew exactly what they are paying for. She tried to make some more money selling fruit. But, to make a profit at that, she would have had to cheat on her scales. She would not do that, so she lost her investment.

Some true-believing Catholics may be devoted to the world of God because they have no opportunities to enter the world of commerce even if they wanted to. To some extent, though, their glorification of the world of God may inhibit them from taking full advantage of the market even when they get the chance. Their missionaries transmitted a faith that sacralized and idealized the circumstances of rural life, that respected simplicity and accepted poverty. It encouraged them to seek their dignity not by acquiring personal wealth but by participating in the spiritual and material riches of the Church. In the Church's imposing buildings and solemn liturgies they could see themselves rich and glorious. If they were in need, the Church would provide aid for them. They say that their missionaries were wealthy men—according to one Catholic, the missionary who originally converted his village was one of the richest men in France—who gave up everything to bring the gospel to China. In short, the faith professed by the most devout rural Catholics, at least in the concentrated Catholic enclaves of north China, encourages dependence, sanctifies poverty, and enjoins moral simplicity in a complex world. It is almost as out of sync with the new world of entrepreneurial China as with Maoist China.

As noted in the preceding chapter, not all Catholics in the countryside reject modernization. Many of those whom we interviewed are becoming involved in new commercial enterprises, carrying on trade with the city, seeking to get their children a first-rate secular education. Even if they do not completely give up their faith, they usually see themselves as relatively lax Catholics. If they retain some active faith, they pray for forgiveness of the sins they had to commit to get ahead as well as for safety and success in their endeavors. They do not have any alternative, modern religious vision that they could oppose to the dominant conservative one.

As a consequence, perhaps, one can sometimes discern an undercurrent of desperation in the spirituality of devout Chinese Catholics—"darkness is descending on this place." This darkness is more confusing, more insidious than that of political persecution. There, the darkness is outside the holy community, the world of God. Now the darkness pervades it. It especially affects the younger generation. "Parents want their children to go to church," says an old woman in Baodi County, "but the young people won't go. Parents can't do anything about it." According to a middle-aged woman in the same village, "My son is ashamed to go to church. He says, 'I'm just a guy—how can I go to Church?' That generation receives bad influences from society."

Young people always probably were not as interested in participating in Church activities as their elders. The young generation is indifferent, speculates an old man, "because the young generation has the energy to commit sins." As people age and begin to consider their mortality, they develop an increased interest in religion. Many of our older interviewees spoke of how their faith had deepened as they got older. "I have to pray every day," said one old grandmother, "because at my age, I don't have a lot of time left in this world. If I don't pray, how can I meet God?" A sixty-year-old man from Xian County has "a friend who became a Party member in 1958. He made an oath to give up any religion. . . . But, after retiring, he renewed his belief. Now he goes to Church regularly because he can't support his spirit by himself. He worries that God will punish him, and he prays that God will not let him suffer forever." Old people also attend church more frequently for a more mundane reason: they have more free time. A seventy-year-old woman from Baodi says, "All this younger generation has time for is to work, work, work; they don't have time to go to church." A twenty-year-old man from Xian County echoes, "The pressure of life keeps a lot of the younger generation from going to church regularly. Women are not as busy as men so they go to church more often." [15]

Yet the difference between lax youth and pious elders does indeed seem to be increasing. Even in some villages of Xian County, there is a sense of crisis. At a meeting in the town where the cathedral is located, one speaker declared, "Everybody in the younger generation belongs to Babylon!" In less jeremiadian terms, a young woman in Xian County studying to be a nun says, "The younger generation is more lax than the older generation. Some go to church just because they are forced to by their parents. They don't truly believe in God. Sometimes they get to church late and leave early." Why is the new generation so lax? According to the young nun in Xian County, it is "because of TV and alcohol and gambling. Such activities are more attractive." Others cite the pressure of a school education that teaches them "materialism and the theory of evolution." But the young nun also suggests a deeper origin of these temptations—new opportunities for mobility. "Most of the younger generation don't stay at home except during the autumn harvest. After, they all go out to do business. If Catholics work outside the village, they will forget God because there will be no one to remind them."

Finally, the weakening of faith among the younger generation is connected with a weakening ability of parents to influence their children. As true-believing Catholic villagers see it, faith is the glue that holds the generations of a family together. "Faith is the best gift my Mama gave to me," says a twenty-five-year-old nun. This sentiment was echoed by many of our interviewees, women and men. They had gained the faith not from God (which is where Catholic theology says you get it) but from their elders, especially their mothers and grandmothers. Just as

Holy Mary is the person who mediates the individual's connection with God the Father and Jesus the Ruler, the mothers and grandmothers in a Chinese Catholic family do the main work of transmitting and nurturing the faith.

But now almost all parents complain about being unable adequately to control their children. (Everywhere we went, we found parents also saying that they did not want to control their children, that good parents should let their children decide for themselves how to live. Nonetheless, all parents tried to have control.) As one old woman said, "I know that nobody wants to listen to me, so I don't care. I'm old enough to die. I don't have energy to deal with my children." An elderly Catholic leader in Baodi is worried that his generation of pious Catholics "will have no successors."

In some villages, Catholics are trying to overcome the younger generation's laxity by organizing recreational activities for them in the community. In Xian County, we met two elderly men who had just traveled to Tianjin to buy some traditional musical instruments, which they were going to use in organizing a village band. "We are doing this," they said, "because the older generation wants the Church to be attractive to the younger generation. We sense that most of the younger generation has been losing interest in the Church." Other villages were attempting to set up small, village-run businesses that could employ the younger generation of Catholics, thereby keeping them in the village and keeping them in the faith. The lay leader of a Catholic village in Baodi County planned to organize his factory in such a way that the workers could get religious education during their spare time. Some churches have "entertainment halls," where young people can play Ping-Pong and chess and musical instruments rather than watching TV. But as the media and market become increasingly pervasive, such churches will probably be fighting a losing battle.

When villagers leave to work in new jobs in the city or when they aspire to higher education or when they get involved in the complicated business relationships that are the hallmark of modern economic development, they encounter new moral ambiguities that are beyond the horizons of both traditionally educated priests and those local arbiters of righteousness, village gossips. Perhaps the quiet desperation caused by this ambiguity provides an especially fertile ground not only for visions and miracles but for the extreme forms of conflict that have taken place in some Catholic communities.

OBEDIENCE AND FREEDOM

What is at stake in these battles is the capacity of Catholics to achieve a kind of freedom, a sense of having some effective control over their lives. In traditional Catholic teaching, true freedom comes from obedience. To be free is not to do whatever one wants but to follow the will of God. And the will of God is known through the authoritative teachings of the Church hierarchy. Since the Western Enlightenment—and in China since the "Chinese Enlightenment" of the May Fourth Movement—secular intellectuals have found this traditional Catholic claim to be absurd, a transparent excuse for thinly veiled, dogmatic authoritarianism. But many Catholics would find this Enlightenment point of view absurd (one articulate Catholic layman told me that the May Fourth Movement had been a big mistake), not for theoretical but for practical reasons. China's would-be modernizers, the heirs of the May Fourth generation, have not brought Catholics anything that credibly feels like real freedom.

The Communist "liberation" brought them tyranny. One escape from this tyranny, even if it could be realized only within the depths of their hearts, was to maintain their allegiance to the authority of the Vatican and to those bishops and priests who had proved through martyrdom that they were not puppets of the Communist government. Perhaps they have even felt themselves lucky compared with their non-Christian neighbors, who had no such large, glorious alternative structure of authority to counterpose to a powerful, arbitrary, repressive political regime.

With the establishment of a "socialist market economy" under the Deng Xiaoping regime, Catholics have found themselves offered another kind of freedom, which is supposed to compensate for the strictures of an authoritarian government—economic market freedom. While this market freedom may be tempting to some young Catholics, especially those in suburban villages with access to well-developed urban markets, it may not seem significant to many others. First, since villages with a strong Catholic atmosphere have not produced loyal Communist party cadres, they may now lack the connections necessary to attract investment capital—especially in those areas of China where few villagers have migrated overseas, which could provide alternative sources of capital—and thus such communities get relatively few benefits from the market economy.

Second, especially from the point of view of the adult generations, villagers lose a significant degree of social freedom, especially the capacity to control their family lives. In particular, parents feel they are losing control of their children. For rural people who depend on filial sons and obedient daughters-in-law to take care of them in old age, loss of control over one's children amounts to a loss of control over one's life.

But, unlike non-Christian peasants, especially in the hinterlands, who are similarly losing control over their lives while failing to get many benefits from the new economy, Catholics have an alternative. By stressing obedience to the teachings of the Church, parents think they can raise obedient children and thus achieve for themselves the only autonomy worth having, the capacity to organize one's family and to ensure a coherent course of life. Obedience to the Church may bring them a tangible economic freedom as well as this social freedom. Funds available now from foreign sources may be channeled through the Church—funds that may help some communities not only rebuild places of worship but also establish clinics and schools and even local industries.

And, in the Chinese context, a profession of obedience to the pope and to the bishops appointed by him actually leads to a high degree of religious autonomy. In the name of obedience to the pope, one can withhold obedience to those local religious authorities under the control of the Chinese Catholic Patriotic Association and the Religious Affairs Bureau. At the same time, there is no way to receive any regular authoritative instructions from the Vatican. So, for most practical purposes rural Catholic communities are free to organize their religious life in ways that they themselves see fit. The relatively few foreign priests who have had a chance to observe rural Catholic communities in China, especially those connected with the underground, often report modes of worship that seem highly unorthodox—quasi-magical practices of healing and exorcism, for instance, that seem to owe more to folk religion than to Catholic doctrine.[16] And as we have seen, in the name of obedience to a pope who cannot transmit any instructions, many underground bishops and priests are able to act with great independence. Because of the ambiguities within the Church hierarchy, even Catholics associated with the official Church have great freedom to pick and choose which authorities they want to listen to.

THE CATHOLIC VOCATION

For people who claim to have received a vocation to become priests and nuns, the paradoxical connection between obedience and freedom becomes not simply a fact of ordinary experience but a central organizing principle of their spirituality—their way of understanding and justifying the meaning of their lives. This vocation (*zhaojiao*) is spoken of as a mysterious gift of God. Yet vocations follow distinct sociological patterns. They are concentrated in particular kinds of villages and particular kinds of families. The young priests, seminarians, and nuns whom we interviewed in or around Zhangzhuang, the center of the Xian County diocese, almost all came from strong, true-believing Catholic families in strong Catholic villages. Several of them mentioned that their small village (typically, fewer than a thousand people) had produced three or four priests and sisters. Big cities like Shanghai no longer produce many vocations. Their seminaries and convents are filled with candidates who come from the rural hinterlands.

Most, but not all, of the seminarians and postulants (young women preparing to take vows as nuns) said their parents had encouraged them in their vocation. In strong Catholic communities, contributing a son or daughter to the religious life has been a source of pride and status for the family, even during the Cultural Revolution, when some families were persecuted by Red Guards for having produced priests and nuns. However, parents encourage their children to enter religious life only under certain conditions. The most important of these is that the family's needs for continuity be met. Thus, at least one son must marry and produce offspring. A forty-six-year-old mother from Xian County who has a daughter who is a nun and has a son in the Shanghai seminary says, "I support my children serving God. I am not against my children choosing that way." But she is not worried about the continuity of her family "because I have another, older son who already has two sons." None of the priests and seminarians whom we met was an only son. Nor were most of the nuns only daughters. It is useful for families to have at least one daughter who can bring in a bride price that can partially offset the costs of setting up a household for their married sons. It is my impression that most of the nuns we met were "surplus" daughters. (The source of vocations may dry up if the government's one-child policy is strictly enforced. But in Xian County, as in most rural counties, many families, non-Catholic as well as Catholic, ignore or contravene the official birth-control policies.)

As long as a true-believing Catholic family has more sons or daughters than it needs, it will likely encourage the desire of one of its children to become a priest or nun. It seems to be the policy of the Xian County diocese, at least, to pay all expenses for seminarians and postulants so as not to impose any burden on the parents of these aspirants to religious life. Although the priest or nun is in a sense lost to his or her family, in places like Xian County children who become priests and nuns will probably stay fairly close by and will be able to give practical help to their families as well as enhance their families' status.

Yet, even though family and community circumstances may have an important influence on a young person's decision to become a priest or sister, that decision is experienced as an individual choice, a response to a personal calling from God. When asked how he knew he had a vocation, a twenty-year-old seminarian tells a story that seems typical. "It is very complicated. Society is not very good. Morals are corrupt. People can't get a good education, so it is easy for them to become evil. For instance, the laws of the country should control people's actions, but sometimes judges and the police take bribes from criminals. The law has lost the capacity to punish criminals. . . . Because of this, most Catholic families don't let their children leave their village because they worry the children will receive bad influences. . . . Several years ago, I went to Tianjin to do business and rented a stall to sell clothes. I was there a year. But I felt that society was no good. I felt tired. After that I started going to church, and I became a seminarian." Like other seminarians we interviewed, he felt particularly connected with the world of God that was his fervently Catholic village and particularly disgusted with the corruption of the outside world. Yet, he still wanted to leave home. After some disappointing experiences, he found that he could leave home and remain within the world of God only if he accepted a calling from God to be a priest.

This decision let him feel both independent—personally called by a transcendent God—and connected to his family and his community. This sense of personal empowerment leads seminarians toward religious entrepreneurship. As a seminarian proclaimed at the beginning of the Xian County seminary's Christmas party, "China has a vast land and a huge population. It is a great market for Catholicism. Who will take up this responsibility and obligation? Who will open it up and bring it under cultivation? The Lord has placed this important duty on our shoulders. We will say yes to the Lord."

The spiritual empowerment felt by young men accepting a vocation was stronger than that felt by young women who were becoming nuns. Somewhat typical was the story told by a lovely nineteen-year-old postulant. After completing her junior high school education, she got a job in a bank in the local township. It looked as though she was going to be

able to move beyond the narrow confines of village life. But the bank
went bankrupt, so she returned to her village. Then she decided that she
had a vocation to the convent. Accepting the vocation was to submit to
the will of God. When she was an infant, she had been seriously sick.
Her mother prayed, "God's will be done," and she recovered. When she
was five years old, she almost drowned. Once again, her mother prayed,
"God's will be done," and she survived. "I have lived until now," she
says, "because of God's help. So I think that my life belongs to God."
She has gained a kind of independence from her parents that enables
her not so much to do God's will as to accept God's will. Since she
wants to become a nun, she "must pray more than ordinary people, and
do more good works, and show more obedience to my parents."

Some seminarians have a high school education, many no more than
a junior high school education—often in rural schools, which are noto-
riously bad. The first stage of seminary education consists of a remedial
high school education; subsequent stages provide the equivalent of several years of college and some theology. Compared with most people in
hinterland villages, a young priest seems to be a well-educated person,
and he is accorded considerable respect. Priests travel around the county
on motorcycles. Some get to go to seminaries in Shanghai or Beijing.
Nuns are less mobile. In Xian County, for instance, they work in the
complex of establishments connected with the cathedral, teaching in a
kindergarten, working as nurses in a medical clinic run by the Church,
and sewing and cooking for the priests. Their life reproduces the subser-
vient relations that they are expected to have in family life. Yet even
within these confines the act of accepting a vocation can seem like an as-
sertion of freedom. Says the leader of a Catholic village in Xian County,
"A lot of people wanted to be a matchmaker for my second daughter.
My wife and I planned to introduce her to a prospective family. But she
cried and cried. My wife and I said, 'We have to tell the matchmaker that
the arrangement is off.' We told my daughter that we would do what
she wanted. So she went to the Church to become a nun." "If somebody
asked me to share a 'happy life' [get married], I wouldn't be able to go,"
says a seventeen-year-old postulant. "Serving God is happiness."

Priests and nuns believe that their kind of faith, the faith that sustains
a vocation, is not simply a product of one's family environment but
something that must be actively cultivated by the believer. A young
priest says, "I don't think that a true believer just receives the faith from
parents. A true believer needs to understand what Catholicism is, and
then he will receive it." The steady growth in the ranks of seminarians

Figure 11. Fan Lizhu (left) with young nuns in their clinic. Photograph
courtesy of Fan Lizhu.

and postulants, priests and nuns in rural China testifies that Chinese
Catholicism is more than an ethnicity, an identity ascribed from birth
and passively accepted, and it is more than conformity to the customs
of one's community or the dictates of one's parents. For some, at least,
it is an internalized faith, which must be actively sought by individuals;
and when it is found, it is experienced mysteriously not as a human
achievement but as a liberating gift of God.

It is a liberation not only from the desires of the flesh and the confines
of family and village but from the tyrannies of modernity, which have
been all too strongly experienced by many Chinese Catholics. But modernity, in the form of some combination of a market economy and a
powerful state, is here to stay in China. Most people will agree that it
needs to be softened and humanized: the state must become less arbitrary and more accountable, the market economy must become less ra-
paciously competitive and more responsive to the needs of the weak and
vulnerable. In the rural Catholicism that we have described, however, to
receive a vocation to become a priest or nun—or a devout layperson—
is to reject modernity. The strongest true-believing rural Catholics tend
to be the ones most opposed to all forms of modernization, economic
and scientific as well as political. Would it be possible for Chinese Catho-

lics to develop a strong spirituality and morality that would reform modernity rather than rejecting it—to see the freedoms promised by modernity not as antithetical to the freedom that comes from following the will of God but as incomplete and needing to be fulfilled by that higher freedom? If they cannot, it is hard to see how the Church can make a positive contribution to creating a modern civil society.

CHAPTER FOUR

Urban Catholicism and Civil Society

At communion time during Sunday Mass in Tianjin, the worshipers approach the communion rail as if they were crowding into a city bus. As mentioned in the Introduction, there is a lot of jostling and pushing to get there first. The one force of order is a church worker who scrutinizes every person approaching to receive the Sacrament. He stops people he does not recognize and demands proof that they are Catholics in good standing. (He never stopped me, but he once did stop a Chinese man next to me who claimed, "I am a priest from Indonesia.") The behavior of Catholics inside the church reflects the behavior of urban Chinese outside it. On the outside, the only force of order in a jostling, undisciplined public space is the police, who are concerned not so much with maintaining general order as with preventing the wrong people from getting near sources of power.

Most of the people in the church probably recognize one another by sight (because the same people typically attend the same Mass every Sunday), but, like the citizens in Beijing neighborhoods, in an important sense they seem strangers to one another because they have come into the community by different paths and with different needs, expectations, modes of piety. Elderly men and women in old-fashioned clothing sit on their separate sides of the aisle, chanting and singing in rhythmic harmony—old Catholics, perhaps, whose families have lived for generations in the city. Some worshipers do not participate in the singing but mumble prayers to themselves as if oblivious to the world around them, intensely wrapped in private devotion, as if bearing a terrible burden or a secret joy that they dare share only with God. And then there are the younger people, stylishly dressed, the women sometimes daring to sit with their husbands or boyfriends on the men's side of the church (men never sit on the women's side). Like most urban people, rendered mutually suspicious by a legacy of political repression, urban Catholics are wary about discussing their differences openly. As the Chinese Catholic author Yang Ni has put it, "For most Chinese, faith [is] a highly personal matter and hardly a fitting topic for general conversation." [1]

There are many layers to the urban Catholic community, some more, some less interested in contributing positively to China's modernization. Often people from these different layers do not understand or trust one another; they are afraid to communicate openly. The Chinese Catholic community provides a good example of the difficulties all urban Chinese may face in developing a civil society. To understand such difficulties and to see what resources the Chinese Catholic Church may have to overcome them, we begin by discussing how the different layers of the urban Catholic community came into being, with special reference to the Catholic Church's relationship with the urban middle class.

VARIETIES OF URBAN FAITH

Although in the nineteenth and early twentieth centuries the missionaries directed most of their attention toward the countryside, they did not completely neglect the cities. In large cities like Tianjin, Beijing, Shanghai, and Guangzhou, there are solid Catholic communities, some members of which can trace their origins all the way back to the Jesuit missions of the seventeenth century. (In the diocese of Tianjin, for example, currently about twenty thousand Catholics live inside the city, as contrasted with about eighty thousand living in the city's rural suburbs.)

As an urban middle class began to develop in the early twentieth century, some missionaries began to reach out to them. In Tianjin, for instance, the French Jesuits in 1921 established the College of Commerce and Industry, aimed at the *bonne bourgeoisie* of north China. Recognizing that, "among the upper classes, Catholicism seems to be the religion of the poor and ignorant, in spite of its brilliant role under Kangxi," the Jesuits aspired "to demonstrate to people who take legitimate pride in their ancient civilization and who prize new progress that the Catholic religion is capable of surpassing every other religion in the domain of spiritual culture and moral formation." [2] The college became home to none other than Pierre Teilhard de Chardin, the famous Jesuit paleontologist and theologian whose attempt to reconcile modern theories of evolution with Catholic theology eventually helped to inspire the second Vatican Council's theological acceptance of the modern world. In the 1930s, the College published a weekly newspaper introducing readers to modern developments in science and international affairs. Fu Jen University in Beijing and the Jesuit-run Aurora University in Shanghai carried on similar missions.[3]

Yet the urban middle-class communities cultivated by Catholic missionaries in the early twentieth century were imbued with a different kind of modernity from that cultivated by liberal Protestants and secular reformers. An alumnus of Beijing's Yanjing University remembers, "When we visited the [Catholic] Fu Jen University, we used to say that it was like going from capitalism to feudalism."[4] Established by American liberal Protestants, Yanjing (whose students wore Western suits) had as its motto "Freedom through Truth for Service." It aimed to produce independent, critical intellectuals who could creatively handle the ambiguities of modern Chinese society. The Catholic university (whose students wore Chinese gowns) emphasized discipline and religious orthodoxy and sought to protect its students from the corrupting influences of the larger world. Catholic students were sequestered in special dormitories apart from non-Catholics. The College of Commerce and Industry in Tianjin, which was more conservative than Fu Jen, took great pride in the fact that its students (unlike students from the Protestant and state universities) did not get involved in any of the patriotic movements of the time. The students and ordinary faculty of the College had no idea of the radical ideas being developed by Teilhard de Chardin. It was not the place of ordinary Catholics to explore such matters. Exploration of dangerous ideas was to be carried out only by specially trained and qualified ecclesiastical elites.

In short, the Catholicism preached to the urban middle classes imbued them with aristocratic values: deference to authority, a sense of natural superiority over the lower classes, and a spirit of noblesse oblige, often expressed in an aspiration to protect one's inferiors from harm. Although some Catholics cultivated an appreciation for higher learning, including learning about science and technology, they suggested that such knowledge was only for people who occupied the appropriate rung on the social hierarchy. Properly qualified priests could explore the mysteries of theology and use their knowledge to instruct laypeople. But they should parcel out that knowledge in a way that would not unsettle the simple faith of ordinary laity. While Teilhard was speculating on the divine purposes behind human evolution, his Jesuit confreres were teaching the peasant Catholics of Xian County that the theory of evolution was the essence of godlessness. And laity should never dare to challenge the teaching of the priests. Thus, urban elites could aspire to higher learning and use their knowledge and other privileges to help those poorer than themselves; but peasants should not aspire to become like urban elites.[5]

This elitist version of Catholicism had its resonances with some strands of Confucianism—strands that eventually reappeared in the authoritarian, hierarchical, paternalistic practices of the Communist Party. But such elitism was opposed to the populist thrust of early Communist ideology, which appealed to peasants and workers to overthrow "feudalism and imperialism" and to become masters of the new society. In the name of this ideology the Communists carried out their early assaults against the Catholic Church. In the cities, as in the countryside, government persecution often strengthened rather than weakened a sense of Catholic identity. In cities like Shanghai, old Catholic families tended to live in the same neighborhoods and to be intricately connected through kinship ties.[6] As in villages, the faith of such Catholics was so connected with these primary social ties that it would have been difficult for them to repudiate their faith even if they had wanted to. Persecution, rather, produced martyrs, who inspired the community to deepen its solidarity.

But even as the old Catholics in the major cities were strengthening their Catholic identity, new opportunities in the city were tempting the faith of some rural Catholics. In the early years of the Communist regime, many ambitious young peasants received the opportunity to move to the cities to staff new government offices and new industries. More than any antireligious propaganda, the lure of upward mobility undermined the faith of the Catholics among them. Take, for example, Zhang Xuansun, a former altar boy who became a Party member. He comes from a village several hours by train from Tianjin city. His family is part of one of the biggest and oldest (three generations) Catholic lineages in his village. When he was a teenager, in the 1940s, the local priest was so impressed with his leadership ability—"I can speak with anyone, get along with anyone. If people have problems, they just come to me to solve them"—that the priest invited him to live in the church compound. In the late forties, as political turmoil engulfed the region, the priest left the parish and Zhang left the village. Migrating to the city, Zhang got a job as an apprentice in a small factory. The same abilities that caught the eye of the local priest now caught the eye of Communist Party recruiters. In 1951, he entered the Party, renouncing his Catholicism in the process. His mother, he remembers, was bitterly disappointed. Now, over forty years later, his relatives in the village are still urging him to return to the faith before he dies. But, he says in a heartfelt manner, "I have no regrets." His village and family were too confining, he says. Entering the Party opened up new vistas, opportunities he could never have had in the village.

The sentiments of this sixty-five-year-old former altar boy are echoed by two distant cousins, in their early twenties, who have recently left the same village and also left their faith. Among the few villagers who went to upper middle school, they are recent graduates of a technical college and have gotten jobs that enable them to transfer their residence permits to the city. "As far as my own faith is concerned," says one of them, "I fell away from it in upper middle school, when I lived in the county seat away from my family. If you have hopes of joining the Party, you can't believe. Besides, your family doesn't know what you are doing."

Although of different generations, these former rural Catholics reiterate the same themes. Village life was stifling, confining, stagnant. Catholicism was part and parcel of that life, and, if anything, it reinforced the hierarchies and strengthened the boundaries of their rural communities. Because of their skills, they have the opportunity to leave the confines of hierarchy and community. To take full advantage of the opportunities, they have to rely on the Communist Party. If they had joined the Party while living in the village, they would have been subjected to painful social pressure, not least of all from their own families. Perhaps they could have never risen far in the rural Party organization because their Catholic background would have been held against them. But in the city, the social pressure is minimized. Separated from their village, they can shed their Catholic identity in a way a villager cannot.

But the experience of the elder Zhang was perhaps far more common than that of his younger cousins. In the early 1950s, the Communist regime offered a great many opportunities for mobility for capable men like himself. If one were willing to sell one's soul, one might at least gain an exciting new world. By the late 1950s, however, the Communist regime had solidified into a rigid, static hierarchy. A comprehensive household registration system made it virtually impossible for a peasant to migrate to the city. In the cities, workers found themselves confined to huge work units, which afforded little lateral mobility and made limited upward mobility dependent on political activism and the patronage of one's work-unit superiors. For most city dwellers in this system, the government could provide few rewards. People were kept in place by the Party's and the state's command of an exquisite array of punishments, ranging from restrictions on one's ability to buy the most desired kind of bicycle to long imprisonment in labor camps.[7]

This static hierarchy may have helped preserve a hidden core of faith in many former peasants who had migrated to the city but who, unlike Zhang, were not willing or able to become political activists. In the mature work-unit system, as Andrew Walder has analyzed it, the rewards for activist strategies "are limited and the number of promotion opportunities are few." In this context, workers use defensive strategies to keep the political system at arm's length. "The average worker puts forward the expected facade of political compliance, behind which he or she is relatively free to live a private life."[8]

An example of a Catholic whose faith is maintained through such a defensive strategy is Mr. Wang, introduced in Chapter 1 as the man who had lovingly copied out the chart depicting the Catholic history of the world. He arrived in the city and began work in a factory in 1950, about the same time that Zhang entered the Party. He does not seem to have any of the mental agility and energy of Zhang, however. He appears to have cherished living a quiet life, staying out of trouble. Since he had never called attention to himself, he avoided being persecuted during the Cultural Revolution.

His faith took him out of his isolation in a dead-end job in a lonely city and connected him with the world of meaning in his village. "What I believe is what my parents believed." He is most animated when talking about his village. He still keeps in close touch and seemingly knows about every wedding and funeral that takes place there. The faith also gives him a link with the wider world of the universal Church. After showing us the chart of Church history that he had copied out, he talked about how Catholics in all countries must know about this chart because there are universal standards that all Catholics follow.

Maintained in isolation through a defensive political strategy, his faith is a passive rather than an active faith. He never showed the zeal that would court martyrdom during the Cultural Revolution. "There was no Church, no priest then. So you couldn't pray out loud." People knew that he was a Catholic, but "you just wouldn't speak about it. They wouldn't say anything; you wouldn't say anything." To this day, he refrains from getting involved in the battles that polarize the Church.

"I don't pay any attention to it," he says when asked about the split with the underground Church. "I believe in God, not in priests."

It is a faith well adapted to the city of the late Maoist era—to a time of little social change, much disillusionment, and little hope. As my colleague Fan Lizhu put it, the faith seems to give people like Mr. Wang a *jingshen danwei*—a "work unit of the spirit." Such a faith added private warmth and meaning to the cold, gray public life of the Maoist regime. But it is not a faith capable of giving active meaning to the task of improving society, of accepting yet morally regulating the entrepreneurial energy of the city in an era of market reform.

So far, then, we have seen several different layers in the Catholic community of the Chinese city. The old urban Catholics occupy a rather closed niche in the urban ecology; they are hardened through years of persecution, strong in their ascribed identity, often hostile to the Communist regime, and, through both theology and life experience, not disposed to trust outsiders. The lapsed Catholics from the countryside see their rural faith as incompatible with the opportunities for personal mobility made possible by the Communist-controlled city; sometimes, during the big festivals, some of them sneak into the back of the church (as Zhang's cousins admitted they did), perhaps to rekindle memories of past affiliations. And the coping Catholics, like Mr. Wang, find in the faith spiritual consolation and a personal connection privately achieved within a hostile environment.

These layers do not seem a fertile source for the development of the social capital necessary for a civil society. The old Catholics are like what the sociologist Herbert Gans called "urban villagers." They have a great deal of internal solidarity but are too clannish to cooperate effectively with outsiders, even with Catholics from outside the city, not to mention non-Catholics. (Although some Catholic priests and Protestant ministers speak of a deepened mutual respect and understanding coming out of their experience of suffering together in labor camps,[9] there seems to be little ecumenical cooperation at the grass roots.) Perhaps, too, the old Catholics are too deeply invested with the hierarchical vision of Church and society that early-twentieth-century European missionaries taught them. Because they have had to suffer so much to maintain the purity of their identity and because that identity is so connected with loyalty to a hierarchical church, some of them are obsessed with questions about the legitimacy of their bishops, which keeps them from making constructive efforts to find adequate leaders under inevitably ambiguous circumstances. And Catholics like Mr. Wang, deeply touching as their piety may be, seem too passive, too risk-averse, too focused on personal salvation to creatively meet the challenges of modernity.

THE CHALLENGE OF MODERNITY

Perhaps the inability of these layers of the Church to adapt to a new urban situation is responsible for a decline of vigor in Catholic communities in China's biggest cities. Churches were first reopened in the early 1980s in large cities like Shanghai and Beijing, and Catholic life seemed to have begun its revival there. By the mid-eighties, these churches were packed. In Shanghai and Beijing the most important seminaries were reestablished. Thanks to help from foreign churches, especially in Hong Kong and Taiwan, these seminaries now have good libraries, and some courses, which introduce students to the thinking in theology and morality inspired by Vatican II, are taught by distinguished experts from Hong Kong and Taiwan. The first seminarians in these national institutions came from the cities in which they were located. But now these institutions have few seminarians from the city. The countryside is producing most applicants for the priesthood. Moreover, attendance at the big cathedrals, like the Jesuit-run Zikawei, in Shanghai, and the South Church, in Beijing, has been declining.

Bishop Aloysius Jin Luxian, the bishop of Shanghai (recognized by the official Church), writes:

> To tell the truth, I had no fear for our Catholics facing the challenge of persecution. But, now, facing the challenge of modernization, of pure materialism, of the idolatry of money, of individualism, I have fears. How to teach the Catholics to live the Gospel? How [should] we ourselves live the Gospel in the quickly changing China? . . .
>
> I had no fears forty years ago, for our Catholics were educated in our Catholic schools. They were better prepared to resist all kinds of challenges. The parish was the center of their lives. Many were ready to sacrifice everything for keeping the faith.
>
> But, now, all Chinese grow up in the atmosphere of atheism. Education belongs to the Party. It is the Party's monopoly. Parish activity is reduced only to the religious service, to brief homilies, and short catechism on Saturday evening and Sunday morning. Children's homework is so heavy that they have very little free time. . . . All adults talk mostly about money, business, stock market, speculations. Every family has a TV set. They watch TV through the satellite; they watch videocassettes imported from Hong Kong, Taiwan, and America. They play cards and mahjongg. The youth goes to cinema, to theater, to karaoke. They find little time to pray. They go to the

church but they begin to find the Latin Mass unintelligible and too long. The new civilization rises, the new era comes. How to evangelize under these circumstances? [10]

The bishop evokes a time when the old Catholics of Shanghai truly lived in a world of God, with its own educational system and centered on a neighborhood parish. Such a Catholic community grew even stronger under the pressure of persecution. But now the old Catholic district is no longer intact; urban development is rapidly changing the face of Shanghai and the old Catholic district is located on prime real estate.[11] The community no longer has its own schools to socialize its youth. Scattered throughout a secular, skeptical society, young Catholics do not have a deep enough understanding of their faith to answer the questions of nonbelievers. Accustomed to bolstering their faith with the social support of a self-enclosed community, Catholics lack the inner direction necessary to sustain the faith. Other Catholic communities in the United States and Europe have surmounted some of these challenges, but doing so has taken many decades and has required a redefinition of faith and a reform of liturgy that the Shanghai Church has not had time to accomplish. The bishop almost seems to long for the days when persecution strengthened the faith.

Catholics like Mr. Wang who came to the city in the past several decades, lived separate from the enclaves of old Catholics, and clung to a private faith in a gray world are also threatened by the new situation. Their faith was sustained partly because the rest of the world was so bleak. Hours of prayer—and, after the reopening of the churches, hours spent at Mass—were a blessed relief from the tedium of underemployment in dead-end jobs and the boredom of a city where there were few opportunities for recreation of any kind. Now, as the old state industries shed workers, people have to scramble to find new opportunities, and TV, movies and karaoke are added distractions in a harried life.[12]

It is not that the Church does not recognize the problems of an incipient market economy. "Since the economic reform in China and the transition from central planning to free market," says Bishop Jin, "we are witnesses of a quick change of mentality, of ideology of most Chinese—from Marxism to consumerism. Traditional moral values disappear. Hardworking spirit diminishes. The stability and harmony of the family is reduced, the farmer leaves the land and rushes to the large city. A new era, a new period, begins. The new rich are praised, honesty is rather neglected, one runs to speculation, falsification of products." [13]

This diagnosis of the moral problems of the new market economy is commonplace, its truth patently obvious not just to Catholics but to almost everyone in China. As a non-Christian intellectual put it to me, "One big difference between now and the early Cultural Revolution era is that back then no one had doubts. Now everybody doubts everything." But the Church does not have a credible solution to this problem. The intellectual whom I have just quoted visited a Catholic church and was impressed with the singing and the devotion of the people. "I would have considered becoming a Catholic," he said, "if it weren't for the sermon. The priest has nothing to say." Intellectual arguments alone, of course, are not able to produce change. But, whether the Chinese Catholic Church's message is delivered through sermons or liturgy or simply through the attitude of the clergy and the most devout laity, it sometimes seems that the only answer that the Church can give to spiritually troubled city dwellers is to retreat to an enclave of Catholics isolated from the world and centered on the parish—a world of God that can no longer exist.

Rather than being an institution that a dominated working class clings to in defiance of persecution, the urban Church is challenged to become an institution that an emerging middle class will seek out in spite of distractions. This challenge will yield a different style of belief and practice than has existed up to now. If it emerges, this new style will undoubtedly evolve more through lived experimentation than through any systematic reflection and organization. There are small signs that the evolution is fitfully occurring.

One example I found in my research was Miss Xia, a divorced, single parent with an eight-year-old daughter; raised as a Catholic in a Catholic village, she had moved to Tianjin and sells vegetables in a market. There is a lot of unkind gossip about her in her village—that she is an immoral, indecent woman because of the way she divorced her husband and left home. Interviewed in the tiny room she rents next to the market, she did not seem so indecent. But she did seem unusually independent and ambitious.

In her telling, she left her husband because he was lazy. "If he had one extra yuan in his pocket, he wouldn't do anything—just sit around the house, smoking and drinking." But she wanted a better life. If she saw other people getting more material possessions, she wanted them too. So she got divorced from her husband, left the village—"If I stayed, I would have had to marry another farmer"—and is seeking a better life among the floating population of the city. She does not have an urban residence permit but earns enough cash selling vegetables to take care of her basic needs. She is on the lower edges of an emerging class of independent petty entrepreneurs.

Unlike Mr. Wang, who was a devout Catholic when he came to the city and who struggled to cling to his faith through many hard years, Miss Xia was a lax Catholic. (Since she did not bother to get her marriage blessed by the Church, she has not broken any of the laws of the Church by getting divorced.) But, for her, the city has been an inducement to faith, not an obstacle to it. In her description, she has now become a devout believer. In the village she had received only an informal baptism from her mother. Now, in the city she has undergone a formal baptism by a priest.

Though she "believes much more strongly than when I was in the village," she "commits many more sins." The sins are mainly "economic sins." Everyday she commits such economic sins by rigging her scales so that people are getting less than they think. "You have to be realistic when working in the market. If you don't cheat people, you'll never make any money." Unlike the Catholic villagers of Xian County who stay resolutely within the world of God, shunning commercial endeavors, she is willing to confront the moral ambiguities of the market economy. Her religion does give her some moral restraint, however. "Because I believe in God, I don't cheat everybody. If I see people who are especially poor or pitiful, I won't cheat them so much. But my first principle is that I don't lose out. And if a customer looks too arrogant, I'll cheat them more."

People at the church in Tianjin have been kind to her and perhaps have even given her a little financial help when she needed it. But she seems to go to church more for spiritual and moral support than for any financial benefit. "People there are very concerned about you. They want to teach you doctrine." The Church also gives her a sense of peace. "According to Catholic teaching, everyone has a cross to bear. My cross is too heavy. But I made it myself. . . . Often when I feel bad, I go to the church to free myself."

In this confessed sinner, we can see the tentative emergence of a new kind of urban Catholic identity. This identity is voluntarily assumed; it is not based on membership in rural or urban corporate groups, but centered on the acceptance of individual responsibility—"My cross is too heavy. But I made it myself." It is an identity of entrepreneurs striving to take advantage of opportunities for mobility and prosperity opened up by a market economy. It is an identity vulnerable to loneli-

ness, confusion, and anguish because of the moral ambiguities of modern
commercial relations and consumer society. Miss Xia, at least, is too
enthralled by the promise of new urban opportunities to consider renouncing them. In this new context, a desire for mobility out of the confines of village life leads people like Miss Xia into the Church rather
than away from it. Amid the alienation, insecurity, and anomie of modern urban life, the Church provides a place where some people can find
others who care about them, some fixed moral reference points, which
are satisfying even though unattainable, and a sense of transcendent
meaning that can give them a measure of peace.

Miss Xia does not want to be a heroic Catholic. At least for her, the
battles between the Patriotic Association and underground priests seem
irrelevant. She wants spiritual consolation and companionship and
comes to the church because the liturgy and doctrine promise them.
Getting involved with the politics of the Patriotic Association and the
underground Church is not a path to spiritual consolation, so she avoids
it. Without rejecting the ideals sustaining a spirit of martyrdom, she sees
herself as a sinner, inspired by, even redeemed by, those ideals, though
unable to achieve them. Perhaps, in her all too fallible human struggles,
she begins to provide some of the necessary bridges between the anti-
modernist, ethnic Catholicism of the rural past and a new, open, volun-
tarist urban Catholicism. The challenge of the Church's leadership will
be to articulate a theology and to develop a sacramental life that can give
meaning and support to this experience.

THEOLOGICAL RENEWAL

In the cities, younger, better educated Catholics may not yet have personally experienced all the disappointment and hope Miss Xia has experienced as a consequence of the new social fluidity, but they are better
able intellectually to anticipate this fluidity and ponder its implications.
Outside every Mass at the Tianjin cathedral, a group of men and women
in their early twenties, some of them university students, sell Catholic
literature: introductions to the "new Mass" of the second Vatican council, new hymnals for worship, updated compendia of Christian doctrine,
and even sophisticated books about the history of Chinese Catholicism,
like a translation of Jonathan Spence's *The Memory Palace of Matteo
Ricci*.[14] Some of them complain that too many priests and too many
laypeople cling too tightly to outdated theologies and styles of worship.
The various Masses at the cathedral have different styles. The 7:30 Mass

on Sunday morning is a traditional Latin high Mass, which the priest says with his back to the people. But the Mass at 7:00 in the evening is in Chinese, in the Vatican II style. It attracts a noticeably younger congregation than the traditional morning Mass. All this points to the fitful emergence of an updated Chinese Catholicism, better able than in the past to grapple with the problems of modernizing China.

To date the most subtle reflection on the nature of the new spirituality needed in the new situation—and on the obstacles to achieving it—comes not from a theologian or even a priest or nun. It comes from the lay Catholic short-story writer Yang Ni, who is currently pursuing graduate studies in Europe.[15] His story "Longqi: Dragon Prays" has the feel of autobiography. Its eponymous hero was raised in a Catholic village, travels to Beijing to attend a university, eventually goes abroad to both Europe and the United States for graduate education in religious studies, and finally decides to become a priest and return to China to serve the Church there. Each stage of his journey is marked by a sometimes painful refiguring of his faith.

His parents belonged to the underground Church, which he attended because "he had always been a dutiful son and obeyed his parents' wishes." Consisting mostly of family and kin and meeting surreptitiously in private homes, the group had an intense solidarity—too intense for Longqi. "The 'underground' church community was indeed like a closely knit family. He felt, however, that the underground Church inserted right in the middle of China's large family of one billion people made for an overdose of family spirit."

When he begins to question even small points of Church practice, his parents tell him, "Don't ask too many questions and keep on saying your prayers." Partly to escape the excessive "family spirit" of the local underground Church, he slips into an official Church during Mass. Although he is alert to the possibility "of finding some evidence of the 'devils' that were said to inhabit these 'official' and 'patriotic' churches," the official Church is appealing because its religious services have more solemnity and grandeur than the underground. Also, the official Church has more of the hierarchy that he regards as essential to Catholic faith. From his parents he had learned that priests and nuns were "above the pains and angers, the pleasures and joys of life. . . . Chinese Catholics tended to put them on pedestals, like sacred statues of Our Lord and Our Lady." But, in the underground gatherings, the priest sometimes wore just ordinary work clothes instead of cassock and vestments. He did not fit Longqi's image of what someone with priestly status should look like.

When Longqi goes to the university he adapts to the repressive polit-ical atmosphere of the city and hides his faith from his fellow students. "However, he couldn't disguise his nervousness whenever he walked out of the school-gate to go to Sunday Mass. He was fearful that a fellow student or teacher might stop him and ask where he was going. It would be awkward for him if one of his fellow students were to discover that among their number there was someone who feigned indifference but really did have an interest in religion." The urban Church itself reflects this atmosphere of repression. Longqi is taken aback by the coldness of the urban Church. When he arrives at the gate of the church, a porter demands to see a letter of introduction from the Religious Affairs Bu-reau and other proof that Longqi is truly a Catholic. "Longqi felt mis-erable. He was from a small town and couldn't imagine how a repre-sentative of a sacred institution like the church could treat visitors with such coldness. This incident only caused him to become even more reticent and circumspect whenever he went to church." He nonetheless secretly holds on to his faith. Individually clung to, rather than socially supported, his faith is that of a defensive Catholic, a private glint of meaning and a link to the warmth of family in a cold and constricted world.

When he gets a chance to study abroad, it is "like escaping the bird cage." He is grateful, finally, for the chance to express himself, to openly say what he thinks and feels without having to worry about censure from his family or political surveillance in the city. "Now that he was abroad, Longqi no longer had to wear dark glasses when he went to church, and he no longer felt afraid that he'd run into an acquaintance along the way who might ask where he was going." He is disturbed, however, by the lack of hierarchy and formality in the Church in Europe and the United States. The Catholic faith has always given its believers a sense of place in a vast chain of being that situates one in a sacred his-tory and a sacred cosmos. For Longqi, this chain was still imagined in terms of the Counter Reformation Catholic Church's ecclesiastical hier-archy. He could not imagine how the faith could provide the same sense of meaning while presenting itself in egalitarian terms.

> One Sunday, by chance, he found himself at a very strange Mass. It was in English; people were strumming on guitars and singing hymns in American country style folk music.
> He couldn't respond to the Sign of Peace, not just because it was said to him in English, but because people were shaking hands and some were even embracing each other. Then, just as he was about to receive Communion, he

was startled to see that the host was made of coarse, brown bread. He left feeling that the atmosphere was just a little too warm for comfort. He never went back to that strange church again.

When Longqi discovered that in Western churches lay people were allowed to distribute Holy Communion, he felt that showed a daring bordering on the extreme. . . . If lay people took over this task, what was left for priests to do? . . . And, he wondered, whatever happened to "reverence for holy things"? This, he was sure, would be his mother's comment when she heard about such goings on.

When he returns home on vacation, he has to repress his new ideas. He does not dare tell the village Catholics about the changes he has witnessed abroad. When he timidly hints at some of these changes, a village Catholic snarls at him, "How can the Church change? . . . You're another one of those university students and a pagan to boot."

Longqi's challenge is to develop a faith that fits the experience of graduate students in Western universities and would meet the aspirations of the new middle classes, especially the incipient professional class in China: a faith that would allow one to think critically, cope with ambiguity, take initiative, constructively interact with a wide variety of people, and be committed constantly to broadening one's worldview. At the same time, he desires a faith that will enable him to maintain his loyalty to those primary ties of family and community that nurtured that faith in the first place. Finally, he makes a breakthrough.

Longqi thought of his grandmother; . . . he could never understand how his grandmother always found time to say her Rosary. He himself prayed rarely. He did go to church regularly on Sundays but could seldom fathom why. Probably more from habit than anything else. As long as things were going smoothly in his life, he seldom bothered with religious devotions. . . .

Longqi's grandmother often appeared in his dreams. He began dreaming of her from the moment he left China and even more so after she had died. He'd awake from these dreams feeling miserable and alone. They made him question why good people had to die, while the evil lived on in relative peace. On one occasion, when such thoughts were more persistent than usual, he opened a Bible to the Book of Job and began to read. Suddenly he felt his whole world changing. In the past, he had hoped to reassure his grandmother that she need not worry about the Thunder God setting her house afire with lightning and burning it down; now he fully realized that his grandmother's house had indeed caught fire and burned to the ground. She was now gone and Longqi felt an urgent need to pray, to talk with God again. For the first time in a very long time, he knelt on the floor in the middle of the day and prayed. He did not know for how long he stayed kneeling there, but eventually he rose to his feet. Then he went off to take a shower to celebrate his rebirth.[16]

The story of Longqi begins with a quotation from I Corinthians, "When I was a child, I spoke as a child and acted as a child. Now that I have grown up, I have put away the things of a child." Longqi's journey is a passage to adulthood. From a faith that is identified with village and family, he progressed first to an internalized but defensive faith and finally to a dynamic, active faith. After living in a childhood world where all was black and white—where underground priests were saints and official Church priests were devils—he developed an appreciation for ambiguity and finally a willingness to seek out goodness in places where it does not seem apparent. From the intense, primary, but deeply hierarchical solidarities of a village Catholic community, he progressed first to the cold but capacious hierarchies of the open cathedrals of the official Church and finally to an appreciation for the humanity and the responsibilities of all members of the Church, whether clergy or laity. His "grandmother's house" has burned down. But he now has an adult faith that connects him in a new way to his grandmother, his family, his village, and the people of China.

As the story depicts it, it takes a great personal struggle for Longqi to achieve his "adulthood." And, at the end, certain doubts remain. Longqi is concerned that his growth toward a universalistic understanding of Christianity is contrary to traditional understandings of filial piety. Finally, he affirms that his new faith is not a denial but a sublimation of filial piety, a calling from his True Father in heaven. But he knows that his old friends would accuse him of being "Westernized," of deserting his Chinese roots. One senses that he will constantly have to rethink and reaffirm his faith in the face of this accusation throughout the rest of his life.

THE CHURCH: A RESOURCE
OR AN OBSTACLE FOR CIVIL SOCIETY?

The story insightfully points to the kinds of religious evolution that would have to occur if the Catholic Church is to be meaningful to a young, educated, urban Chinese middle class. If this growth did take place widely, the Catholic Church might make a strong contribution toward constructing moral underpinnings for a modernizing China. There are, however, significant obstacles, which have their origin not simply in the internal life of the Church but in the large centrifugal forces that are pulling China apart. The Church not only reflects these problems but in some respects exacerbates them.

First, uneven economic development leads to widening gaps between coastal cities and the Chinese interior. Especially in the hinterlands, there is a stark gap between city and countryside, which creates great differences between urban and rural religious experience. As explained in Chapter 3, the most staunchly Catholic communities are in poor rural areas, but the rural sector of the Church is not going to be easily changed by cultural diffusion from the cities. Because of the development of the underground Church, the differences between urban and rural Catholicism could get wider. If priests like Longqi receive a modernized education—and I have indeed met some like Longqi getting advanced training in U.S. seminaries—they will have a difficult time communicating with the vast majority of Chinese Catholics. As a result, the leadership in parts of rural China might fall increasingly to young priests from the underground Church. In the first seven months of 1994 alone, the underground Church ordained seventy-one priests. As noted in Chapter 1, the training received by such new priests is usually not so much an academic education as a personal apprenticeship to an older priest.[17] In some respects, though, such newly ordained underground priests may have a practical folk piety that makes them more at home with rural life than does the academic education of the officially open seminaries. Differences among the new generation of priests trained clandestinely and those trained in open seminaries could exacerbate differences between an urban, forward-looking Church and a rural, antimodern one.

A second problem is the rapidity of social change in China. The dislocations produced by a sudden transition from a planned to a market economy and the dazzling possibilities opened up by an average 10 percent growth rate force people suddenly to confront important questions of meaning and morality. Bishop Jin referred to many of them. "We feel very weak and powerless against the tide of modernization that brings a lot of products like corruption, idolatry of money, spiritual vacuum."[18] If the Church could give a reasoned, consistent answer to these problems, it might indeed help fill the spiritual vacuum. But throughout the world Catholics are debating how to respond to modernization. To what extent can Catholics accept the logic of capitalism? What should the relationship be between the Church and politics? Should the Church change its doctrine to make it relevant to modern culture? Debate over such questions, which has been going on openly at least since the second Vatican Council, has led to a sharp polarization between "traditionalists" and "modernists" throughout the Church. In the U.S. Church, for example, the supporters of the Chinese underground Church tend to be traditionalists, and supporters of the official Church, modernists. However, in the United States and other Western countries the polarization has developed gradually enough that it produces tension—sometimes strong tension—rather than tumultuous upheaval. In China, people confronted with sudden rapid change have to take sides quickly while being given opposing messages from well-meaning, outside Church members. When the Church in the West catches cold, that in China catches pneumonia. Polarization leads to a potentially life-threatening confusion rather than to an uncomfortable—and perhaps even constructive—tension.

A final problem afflicting everyone in China is the climate of fear and the culture of mistrust that are the consequences of the political repression a corrupt government continues to use to maintain its power. In an effort to weaken the Church, the government has deliberately sown fear and mistrust in the Church. It is widely assumed that both the underground Church and the official Church are infiltrated by the secret police. Many Catholics suspect that at least some of the conflicts between the underground Church and the official Church are fomented by the police to keep the Church divided. Everyone knows that the Religious Affairs Bureau is constantly attempting to manipulate the Church to conform to government purposes. The Catholic Church has been subject to more of this kind of government attention than most groups within Chinese society. Inevitably the level of fear and mistrust within the Church becomes no lower and probably becomes higher than in the larger society. Tensions within the Church can decrease the social trust necessary for the development of a civil society.

Yet the Church is not without resources for overcoming these societywide problems. These resources are above all spiritual: a fundamental message of love, forgiveness, and reconciliation. Leaders like Bishop Jin emphasize this message. "Every day we pray with confidence to the Father in the words our Savior taught us: 'forgive us our trespasses as we forgive those who trespass against us.'. . . Forgiveness and reconciliation are characteristics of Christians for life. One can't imagine a true disciple of Jesus who stubbornly refuses pardon and reconciliation with his brother and sister." [19] Some loyalists from the underground Church accuse official Church leaders like Bishop Jin of being tools of the government and hypocritically using the message of reconciliation to weaken the heroic loyalty of true Catholics to the pope.[20]

But Bishop Jin's position is reinforced by the pope himself. Speaking in Manila, where he had traveled for the celebration of the Tenth World

Youth Day, in January 1995, Pope John Paul II stressed the theme of reconciliation. Although, in an indirect word of encouragement to the underground Church, the pope emphasized that "a Catholic who wishes to remain such and to be recognized as such cannot reject the principle of communion with the successor of Peter," he said that he had received "many testimonies of faith from communities throughout China" in a way that suggested (with typical papal indirection) that these communities are not confined to those associated with the underground Church. He ended his message with an exhortation to all "to seek paths to communion and reconciliation."[21]

Bolstered by such authoritative direction, different parts of the Church might indeed strive toward mutual understanding and reconciliation. Cooperation in material projects could further help them achieve this spiritual goal. For instance, urban Catholics of all kinds are united in wanting to retrieve from the government more of the property that had been confiscated during the Maoist era; and they are eager to work together to rebuild and refurbish church buildings. Participation in this common work can lead to mutual learning and a spirit of solidarity that overcomes differences. Remember, from Chapter 1, that in some places the underground Church and the official Church have worked together to refurbish a church, and they have worked out cordial arrangements for each to have their Masses there.

In spite of the problems mentioned above—problems endemic to all of Chinese society—I have sensed in Chinese Church celebrations a spirit of collective joy and hope that I have not seen in other contexts. I can empirically document the problems of the Catholic Church in China much better than I can estimate the weight of this sense of joy and hope. But inspired by this sense of hope, I will, at the end of the next and final chapter, speculate on courses of action that the Church could follow if it wished not just to survive or even grow in numbers but to contribute to a humane and decent civil society in China.

CHAPTER FIVE

The Catholic Church and Civil Society

To understand how the Catholic Church, or any kind of association in a pluralistic society, might contribute to the making of a civil society requires more than data about the structure of the group and the character of its members. It requires a larger vision, which will inevitably be influenced by cultural traditions and historical experience, about how different social groups, representing partial, particular interests, can arrive at a legitimate consensus about the public good in a complicated industrial society. There are two major visions of this kind, both deriving from Western political philosophy. (As we shall see, Chinese intellectuals have not even settled on a vocabulary with which to articulate such a vision.) The first, an Anglo-American vision based on thinkers like John Locke, Adam Ferguson, and Adam Smith, mistrusts the power of the state and emphasizes the need of citizens to form associations that are independent of the state. The second, a Continental European vision based on thinkers like Montesquieu and Hegel, has a much more positive view of the state. Only the state can reconcile particular interests in a common, public interest. The state itself must organize and empower the associations of civil society and give them the moral education, the sense of community, and the security necessary for responsible participation in public affairs.[1]

Insofar as one views civil society through the lens of the first vision, one will tend to evaluate the civil status of any social group primarily in terms of its independence from the state. Outlawed groups like the underground Church will be seen as more authentically religious than official groups and perhaps as having more potential for transforming China in a democratic direction. Insofar as one looks through the lens of the second vision, one might be more tolerant of the official Church's acceptance of some government economic support and some government supervision over the choice of bishops.

Traditional Catholic social teaching is in fact closer to this European tradition than to the Anglo-American one. Historically the Vatican has often negotiated concordats under which it accepted support from governments, even governments whose values it did not approve of, in exchange for accepting government input into the choice of bishops.[2] Not only Europeans but also Americans who accept the need of the official Church to reach an accommodation with the Chinese government often justify their thinking by implicit reference to this tradition of thought. This tradition is also culturally congenial to East Asian societies. Countries like Japan and Taiwan base their legal systems on European civil law (German law, mediated through Japan), which in turn reflects the European vision of civil society. Though more paternalistic than most Americans would find tolerable, these political arrangements seem consistent with an effective degree of democratic civic participation.

Yet, however one evaluates the civil status of the Chinese Catholic Church, the actions of that church often lack civil consequences. Within the Chinese Catholic Church—especially the underground Church, but also the official Church—a great deal of organized activity takes place that is independent of any effective government control. This activity uses resources from the Catholic community itself rather than from the government, and it is based on a religious and moral vision that owes nothing to the government. However, in the rural hinterlands where the Church is strongest, this independently organized social activity does not necessarily lead toward social self-governance in a pluralistic society. It sometimes leads to fragmentation and, potentially, anarchy. All too often, Catholics belonging to self-governing organizations on different sides of the conflict between the official Church and underground Church show little capacity to resolve their differences. And, even when they have reasonably peaceful relations with non-Catholics, they do not seem to have a positive desire to cooperate with them. Because, in the current Chinese context, the Catholic Church frequently lacks the moral qualities of civility, the government has some realistic basis to fear that such an independent religious organization may lead to a breakdown of law and order.

When those who (consciously or not) draw on the Anglo-American vision of civil society express their hopes for an improvement in the Chinese political system, they focus on the degree to which China's social space is being filled by groups that are truly independent of the government, and they tend to assume that the more such independent groups there are (whether or not the independence is recognized by Chinese law), the more progress China will be making toward becoming a democratic society. They criticize China for violating human rights by constricting the right of people to form such groups. However, they often underestimate the danger of social anarchy posed by the proliferation of these groups. Americans who celebrate the flourishing of the underground Church tend to base their thinking on this tradition.[3] Western human-rights groups that focus solely on the right of religious communities to independently organize themselves and assume that, defined in this way, religious freedom will lead in a benign way to the formation of a civil society are being naive about the potential role of the Church in such a social context.[4]

But neither can the way in which the Chinese government controls, manipulates, and oppresses the Catholic Church be justified in terms of any European, state-oriented view of civil society. It is difficult to form a civil society when confronted with a state that discourages any of the moral qualities of civility. The Communist Party and the Religious Affairs Bureau are arbitrary and sometimes positively brutal. Since the rights and responsibilities of the Church on the one hand and the government on the other are not defined by any impartially enforceable law, the Church is vulnerable to destructive action by unaccountable government officials. Outrage at this harshness and unaccountability make many faithful Catholics suspicious of Church leaders who cooperate in any way with such officials, even when the Church leaders may do so with good intentions, out of an "ethic of responsibility." The only way, it seems, that Catholics can reach an acceptable modus vivendi with the government is through bribing officials not to interfere too much with religious activities. A government that is tolerable only when it is corrupt is obviously not a government that can empower and inspire a responsible civil society.

INSTITUTIONAL DIFFERENTIATION

At least in the rural hinterland, then, the reemergence of the Chinese Catholic Church cannot in any straightforward way be considered a step toward the reemergence of a civil society. Neither, I would argue, can the reemergence of most rural organizations, like local secret societies, clan organizations, and even village associations. The independence of such groups is often both cause and consequence of the fragmentation of the society or the corruption of its government. In the current Chinese context, they are not part of a transition toward social self-governance. This is not to say that in other contexts they could not become a part of an incipient civil society. What keeps them from playing such a role now is not primarily Chinese culture, not some "Confucian authoritarianism." Within a framework of government regulation based on European civil law as mediated through Japan, the Catholic Church in Taiwan and Hong Kong—together with Buddhist, Daoist, and Protestant groups—plays a responsible role in a vital civil society. The relevant difference between Taiwan and Hong Kong, on the one hand, and the mainland, on the other, is not in classical cultural traditions but in the current institutional framework and recent political history.[5]

The very notion of a civil society depends on a separation between economy, polity, and society. "The down-to-earth sociological meaning" of civil society, according to Ernest Gellner, is "institutional pluralism *of a certain kind.*"[6] Civil society requires an efficient, centralized state and a market economy that may be facilitated and guided by the state but without, as Gellner puts it, "depriving productive units of their unity and autonomy." In between such an economy and state, in early modern Europe, a "society emerged which ceased to be segmentary—either as an alternative to the state, as a mode of efficient statelessness, or as an internal opposition to the state or in part its ally—and yet was capable of providing a countervailing force to the state."[7] This is the institutional basis of civil society.

But this institutional transformation has not taken place in mainland China. Consider the history of the Chinese word for society—*shehui.* This word is not found in its present meaning in classical Chinese but was imported into the Chinese lexicon only around the beginning of this century from Western countries through Japan.[8] It was imported into China to denote a new kind of social entity created by late-nineteenth-century economic development. In the coastal, treaty-port cities, shaped by integration into a Western-dominated global market, China's human landscape was becoming differentiated into at least three domains that were based on different principles and functioned relatively independently of one another: the economy (the theoretical understanding of which belonged to the separate science of economics), the polity (to be studied through political science), and society (to be studied through sociology). Civil society, therefore, refers to an aspect of a particular domain, society, within a modern, institutionally pluralistic world.

In the past several generations, both Taiwan and Hong Kong have developed this kind of institutional pluralism, but mainland China has not. There is a centralized state, but it is highly inefficient, not in effective control of many regions of the country, and in many places not able to control the Party bosses who serve as "local emperors" at the village and township level. China's "socialist market economy" is an unstable hybrid, a mixture not only of socialist and capitalist forms but also of modern and premodern forms. It is not just that about half of urban industrial production still takes place in state-run enterprises but that, in the rural hinterlands, economic relations are still deeply intertwined with social and political relations. It is through personal relationships—*guanxi*—that investment capital is acquired and jobs are allocated. Such relationships are often based on kinship and are usually dominated by powerful local emperors. Such a society is still "segmentary."

Often local Catholic congregations are part of this segmentation. In such a context, the Catholic church can still aspire to be a world of God—not a society of God. It is an aspiration to function as "an alternative to the state, as a mode of efficient statelessness, or as an internal opposition to the state or in part its ally." This aspiration is based on memories of the Catholic experience during the earlier part of this century, when the divisions across Chinese society were even deeper than now, when there was no effective national government, and when China was a jigsaw puzzle of local economies, dominated sometimes by warlords and sometimes by foreign imperialists. Funded and protected by foreign patrons, some rural Catholic communities could act like separate commonwealths in the midst of Chinese society.

It was precisely the set of circumstances that made such commonwealths possible that Chinese revolutionaries labored so hard to overcome. It took raw force to bring this fragmented society together and a massive, intrusive state apparatus justified by a totalistic ideology to keep it together. Now that this ideology has collapsed, and factionalism and corruption among the leadership are increasing, some of the old disunity has returned.

China has a long way to go before it devolves into the fragmented chaos of the early twentieth century, but, relative to the tight unity of the early Mao years, it is heading in that direction. In addition to regional divisions, there is considerable fragmentation at the most basic levels.

Much of the social space of rural society is dominated by revived traditional groups—like village and clan associations, as well as traditional religious groups—that have the potential for causing considerable disruption, especially in the poorer regions of China's interior. Indeed, in many parts of the interior, the countryside is seething with discontent. Knowing that they lag far behind more privileged areas, farmers feel that they are not reaping many of the benefits of modernization. At the same time, they perceive increasing corruption among local officials and a general deterioration of morality. These circumstances have spawned peasant riots, in some cases led by charismatic figures who claim to be the next emperor or by the same secret societies that in the Qing Dynasty led the White Lotus rebellion.[9] In other places the old Triad societies are active, building up lucrative trades in drug trafficking and human smuggling.[10]

Local economy, politics, and society are so intertwined in the countryside that the government understandably fears that the underground Church could lead to political instability. The rural Catholic Church has at least the potential of becoming a nucleus of rural rebellion, which would add to these other sources of fragmentation and instability. Even more likely, it may continue to be a locus of passive resistance and insubordination. Some of the Catholics we interviewed seemed nostalgic for a prerevolutionary situation that was from the point of view of China as a whole a disaster. This is a prescription for a return to a chaotic society rather than for the development of a civil society. The prospect of such a return can be and is used by the Party to justify harsh political repression.

THE URBAN MIDDLE CLASS

However, in the large coastal cities and in the ever-widening suburban areas that are the locus of the most vigorous market-driven development in China, there are nonetheless the sprouts of a genuine civil society. They are still just sprouts, though, and Chinese intellectuals have not yet even settled on a word for them. There are no less than four different terms for civil society.[11] The first, *shimin shehui,* literally means "city people's society." Thus, civil society is urban society. It speaks to issues arising from urbanization and industrialization, especially to the challenge of developing a peaceful habitat for the large aggregations of diverse people who make up modern cities.

Another word for civil society is *minjian shehui,* which means "people-based society."[12] In this usage, civil society is organized through the initiative of the people themselves (*minjian*). But the term *minjian* does not connote independence from government. It is taken for granted in mainland China that people-based organizations cannot properly exist without the guidance and supervision of the government. Yet insofar as such people-based organizations are composed of middle-class people, they may have the capacity to maximize self-organization and minimize government manipulation. In the West, civil society has historically referred especially to bourgeois society (civil society is rendered as *burgerliche Gesellschaft* in German), to the society of the urban middle classes as opposed to aristocratic society, peasant society, or proletarian society. Thus, today, mainstream political sociologists in the United States commonly say that democracy depends on civil society and civil society depends on the emergence of a middle class. Although sociologists continue to debate the exact definition of a middle class, the most relevant characteristics of this social formation were nicely summarized by Tocqueville a century and a half ago: "people who, though neither rich nor powerful enough to have much hold over others, have gained or kept enough wealth and enough understanding to look after their own needs."[13] Such people maintain their comfortable standard of living by relying on their own material resources and skills rather than on the patronage of powerful superiors, and their hope for upward mobility rests on the further development of these personal assets. The evidence seems to suggest that countries without a substantial middle class cannot make the transition to democracy.[14]

In China's coastal cities, the institutional framework is right for the development of a middle class and perhaps a civil society. There, minimally effective urban governments are led by people sophisticated enough and aware enough of the exigencies of foreign investment to encourage an expanding, independent market. Out of an increasingly mobile population organizations of entrepreneurs, professional associations, and a variety of "self-help" groups like those associated with the much-publicized women's hotline in Beijing are forming. While all these associations are carefully supervised by the government, they are organized through the initiative of their members and have a significant capacity to set their own agendas. In ideology and organization, they represent the outlooks and interests of two kinds of fledgling middle class: entrepreneurs and professionals.[15]

Their outlooks and interests are not necessarily well articulated or consistent. In general, entrepreneurs want to minimize government regulation and taxes, but they want the government to maintain law and order and political stability. The professionals want freedom to think for themselves, to choose their own workplaces, and to communicate with fellow professionals around the world. Some, like those volunteering for the women's hotline, also want freedom from traditional family and social pressures. But they also want a government that can provide higher, more secure salaries for people like themselves.

If these groups do represent the beginnings of a civil society, however, it is a thin and fragmented one. They are a small fraction of even the urban population; and their position is extremely precarious. They are under constant supervision by government bureaucrats. Their spheres of autonomy—their capacity to earn an income or to go abroad, for example—are dependent on the good will of supervising officials, which must often be gained by paying bribes.[16] Moreover, the interests of entrepreneurs and of professionals (and of different levels of entrepreneurs and professionals) are, as we have seen, divergent. The situation of this fledgling civil society is somewhat similar to that in the 1930s, when a thin, cracked layer of urban, independent businessmen and professionals (much admired by Western observers) formed a patina of liberalism on a society beset with fatal contradictions.[17]

Today's civil society may eventually follow the path of liberal Western societies and become thicker and may set the tone for the Chinese political economy; it may become, as the third Chinese translation of civil society would have it, a *gongmin shehui*, a "citizen's society"—a society of people governing themselves democratically through self-restrained, reasonable, civic discussion in the public sphere. But this outcome is by no means certain—liberal Western societies, after all, followed uncertain, tortuous paths to this point. An urban middle class may not grow fast enough to have much influence on the centrifugal forces represented by angry peasants from underdeveloped regions and by displaced workers. Corrupt officials may choke off genuine entrepreneurial activity. A Party fearful of losing its power may stifle the emergence of a vocal professional class.

CIVIC MORALITY

Even if these institutional developments do occur, however, they might still not be sufficient for the creation of a self-governing society. "Not all of civil society," as Fareed Zakaria says, "is civic minded." [18] As William Sullivan puts it, "Experience strongly supports the observation that while democratic nations contain vigorous civil societies, with commercial vitality and a pluralistic associational life, these conditions alone are not sufficient to support a stable democratic polity. Civil societies can exist and even to some extent flourish under paternalistic or authoritarian regimes, as some East Asian and Latin American countries have shown. But for a fully democratic political culture to take root something more is needed." [19] A civic-minded civil society—one that could sustain a democratic polity—would be, in the fourth translation of civil society, a *wenming shehui,* a "civilized society" where there is widespread diffusion of the virtues of civility: self-restraint, tolerance for diversity, and a commitment to fair treatment for all.

Where are these virtues to come from? Especially in a country like China, where a fragile, nouveau riche middle class is gripped by rampant consumerism and a frenetic scramble to make money, it is difficult to see how the resources for a morality of civility can arise. They might come from morally respected political institutions. Since the Cultural Revolution, however, China's leading political institutions have not been able to inspire much moral respect. Religion could play an important role in instilling the moral discipline and respect for others that a civic culture requires. A foundation for these virtues is found in all the world's great religions, including Confucianism, Buddhism, and Daoism. One reason people come to churches in China is that, for all the problems of religious institutions, they seem, relatively speaking, to be islands of integrity in a corrupt and cynical society. But only a certain kind of religion could contribute to the moral basis of a civil society. Unfortunately, traditional religions, certainly including Christianity, have often been used to justify self-absorption, intolerance, and callousness toward outsiders. The moral challenge facing those who would like to build a viable civic culture is to reformulate old religious and humanistic traditions in a way that can sustain the virtues needed for a humane, modern polity.

To comprehend the challenge facing the Catholic Church, consider once again the characteristics of civic relationships that Robert Putnam enumerates in his study of Northern Italy. Recall that the first characteristic is civic engagement, the expectation that individuals and groups are "alive to the interests of others." A religion that fosters this kind of engagement would have to focus its believers' attention not simply on personal salvation in an afterlife but on the need to make this present world just and humane. A second characteristic is the predominance of "horizontal relationships of reciprocity and cooperation" over "vertical relationships of authority and dependence." A religion that fosters such relationships would have to develop in its adherents a strong, internalized moral authority rather than an authority excessively dependent on hierarchical superiors. A third characteristic is high levels of solidarity, trust, and tolerance. A religion that fosters these virtues would have to respect pluralism; it would not try to use political or social coercion to claim a monopoly over moral teaching. A final characteristic is encouragement of membership in many different, overlapping associations, which moderates and expands loyalties and interests.[20] A religion that fosters such an associational life would have to give up making a total, exclusive claim to its members' identity. It would encourage them to belong to different kinds of groups, many of which would not be connected with the Church. It would not claim that religion gave unambiguous solutions to the issues pursued by political, professional, commercial, and aesthetic groups. It would accept the risk that the loyalties of its believers might be pulled in different directions by these groups, and it would trust that believers with well-formed consciences would determine for themselves how to reconcile these loyalties.

The Catholic Church in China does not fit the description of this kind of religion, at least in the parts of northern China where I did my fieldwork. In this respect, the Chinese Catholic Church is similar to the Italian Catholic Church, which, Putnam argues, "still retains much of the heritage of the Counter Reformation, including an emphasis on the ecclesiastical hierarchy and the traditional virtues of obedience and acceptance of one's station in life"—so that, "at the regional level, all manifestations of religiosity and clericalism . . . are negatively correlated with civic engagement."[21] As we have seen, the Church that was implanted in China in the nineteenth and early twentieth centuries was a typical Counter Reformation Church. It directed the attention of its believers toward achieving personal salvation in heaven rather than trying to change this world in accordance with God's will. It governed itself according to strict hierarchical principles and set forth obedience and humility as the key virtues for lower orders in relation to higher orders. It attempted to gain a monopoly over moral teaching. Although it obviously could not gain such a monopoly in China by allying itself with the Chinese state, it sought to make itself the privileged religion of the French concessions. And, insofar as possible, it grouped its converts into Catholic villages—little worlds of God—where all of social life was dominated by the Church.

Catholicism sustains a way of life that was good for building strong communities in a preindustrial Chinese society but is not good for building a civic morality in an industrialized, urbanized China. In its preaching, the Catholic Church was resolutely opposed to Chinese folk culture. It required its converts to take baptismal names of Western saints. It made them destroy all idols of the folk religion and to give up those rites of ancestor veneration that were central to the Confucian tradition. Yet in its practice it meshed closely with the institutional fabric of the rural society. It celebrated the extended, patriarchal family. It encouraged the localism and particularism of tight-knit village communities. It made hierarchical loyalty to a central (religious) authority a test of the validity of one's faith.

As a result, although it never made large numbers of converts, it was successful in making the Church an integral part of Chinese society. Since the Church was so closely tied to the institutions of rural life, it became as difficult to leave the faith as to leave one's family or to give up one's connection with a native place. Even though many of the first generation in Catholic villages were "rice Christians," brought into the Church by promises of food and perhaps political protection, their descendants often clung tenaciously to their religion throughout the persecutions of the Maoist era and sometimes produced martyrs who displayed a truly heroic faith. The Catholic faith turned out to be strong in some respects because it did not change basic Chinese moral conduct. It adapted itself to and indeed strengthened the major institutions of rural life. It did not make the moral fabric of Catholic rural community different from that of the Big Teaching community. But it inextricably attached itself to particular communities by becoming their emblem of corporate identity. The faith worked like a totem in Emile Durkheim's sociology of religion: not important in itself (even devout believers confess that they "don't know much doctrine"), but vitally important as a sacred marker of the community's identity in relation to other communities.[22] As long as these communities retained their corporate identity—and they were aided in doing so by the Maoist regime's restriction on movement out of rural communities and by the systematic discrimination against Catholics—their faith retained a sacred power, sacred enough that some people would die to protect it even if they did not fully understand it.

The identification with village and family that made Catholicism so durable during the Maoist era may be a liability in the post-Mao era of "reform and opening." Mao celebrated the virtues of rural life, and his policies in effect froze rural communities in place, perpetuating labor-intensive farming and the family and community structures that sustained it. Deng Xiaoping's "socialist market economy" enmeshed rural life in a network of market relations centered on cities and towns. The activism of the most fervent Catholic villages seems to be a conservative reaction against this network. But the tide of market reform is probably unstoppable. As market reform progresses further into China's interior and draws more farmers into an urban political economy, the Catholic world of God may indeed lose its force.

The contrast between the Catholic and Protestant Churches is instructive in this regard. Rural Catholics have been extremely successful in maintaining their identity. The Catholic population has grown from about three million in 1949 to about ten million today. Most of this growth represents natural increase: the communities in place in 1949 have successfully passed their faith on to their children. But the Protestant population has grown spectacularly, from fewer than one million people in 1949 to perhaps twenty million today. Most of this growth has taken place since the early 1980s through new conversions. Some Chinese commentators appropriately speak of a "Protestant fever" sweeping the country.[23]

Although conversions are taking place in the cities, where most Protestants lived before 1949, the hottest part of the Protestant fever seems to be in the countryside. Conversions take place through itinerant lay preachers, most preaching an evangelical Protestant doctrine. It is said that they often demonstrate the effectiveness of their preaching by performing miracles. Often they convert whole villages, which organize themselves through lay leaders around a life of Bible study and worship after the itinerant evangelists move on. Conversion is a search for the new rather than a clinging to the old, a search stimulated and made possible by the new market economy. Although the faith brings no material benefits—apart from the reported miracles—it appears to bring great spiritual consolation to people fearful of the materialism, competitiveness, and corruption of the new society. The Protestants preach a conservative morality, emphasizing the importance of family and community, but their faith perhaps gives them a promise of healing and salvation as they enter the uncharted seas of a new market economy. Moreover, the evangelization of the countryside is made possible by new opportunities for mobility, which allow itinerant preachers to move freely from place to place. One is tempted to speculate that while Catholicism is a way for rural people to shelter themselves from modernity, Protestantism is a way to strengthen and fortify them as they undertake a dangerous pilgrimage into modernity.[24]

Unlike the Protestant Church, then, the rural Catholic Church may have become so tightly integrated into the social world of premodern China that it will not have much that is positive to contribute to market-driven economic and political reforms. Its internal problems exemplify those aspects of China's premodern legacy that continue to bedevil China's reforms: the particularism that makes it difficult to trust those outside one's family and local community, the dependence on hierarchical patron-client relations, and the tendency to be drawn into factional fighting initiated by intrigues at higher echelons of the hierarchy. If the rural Catholic Church continues in its present form into the future, it will be a sign that China's modernization has stalled, that China has not succeeded in giving the market sufficient autonomy from the state and traditional society to allow a civil society to develop. In some important regions of China, at least, the rural Catholic church is like the Catholic church in southern Italy, an institution that reflects and fosters the vertical, insular, familistic relationships that in Putnam's analysis constitute a negative social capital that impedes both economic development and democratic reform.

CATHOLIC REFORM

Although in my view the Catholic church in its present form, with its imagination rooted in the conditions of rural life, may be more of an obstacle than an asset in the creation of a civil society, it does not have to remain that way. Since the second Vatican Council, the Church has undergone profound transformations to adapt itself to the modern world. If some of these changes are accepted by Chinese Catholics, the result could be a Church that is a positive, though critical, force in Chinese society.

How might this transformation take place? To answer this question, we have to turn to Weberian rather than Durkheimian sociology. Max Weber's sociology of religion starts not with religious symbols as emblems of moral communities but with religious ideas that fulfill the human need for salvation. He then investigates how these ideas change and how these new ideas are embraced by certain social carriers, who find the ideas congenial to their social and economic interests. New forms of religious organization are then developed to carry on these ideas.[25]

Since the second Vatican Council, the Catholic Church has been changing some of its ideas. In the Council, the Church authoritatively proclaimed a prophetic new vision about the relation of the Church to the modern world. In effect, it gave up the attempt to create a monolithic world of God backed up by political coercion, dominated by a clerical hierarchy, and excluding nonbelievers. In its Declaration on Religious Freedom, it accepted religious pluralism. While still affirming that the Catholic Church was the bearer of the fullness of divine revelation, the Council recognized the good conscience of those who accepted other religions and the possibility that sincere believers in other religions could find salvation. At the same time, the Church gave up reliance on temporal powers to enforce a monopoly for its message. With the capacity to consider non-Catholics as spiritual equals—not just as people who would at best be eligible for a shadowy limbo after death—Catholics were now set free to work in close cooperation with people of good will outside the Church. In its Pastoral Constitution on the Church in the Modern World, the Council accepted the validity of modern science and much of contemporary philosophy. It encouraged laypeople to use their freedom and reason to seek God's will in secular callings. In its Dogmatic Constitution on the Church, it portrayed the Church not primarily as a hierarchical structure but as a people of God, in which all members had an important role to play and in which decisions should be made on the basis of "collegiality."[26]

Chinese Catholics are only now starting to study the message of Vatican II. Since the mid-1980s, Chinese translations of the relevant documents have been imported, foreign theologians have given courses on the new teachings in Chinese seminaries, and some seminarians have gone abroad to study. As described in the previous chapter, the natural "carriers" of these new ideas are members of the slowly emerging Chinese middle class. Insofar as these ideas become disseminated in China and take hold among an urban middle class, they provide a religious basis for a segment of that middle class to work toward the creation of a civil society. Priests like the fictional Longqi, discussed in Chapter 4, could eventually replace the aging Chinese pastoral leadership, and they could gradually disseminate the new vision to all levels of the Catholic Church.

There are serious obstacles, however. The world-affirming message of Vatican II is not the only Catholic vision being disseminated to China. There is deep division within the universal Catholic Church—not least of all in the United States—about how to interpret and how seriously to take the documents of Vatican II. Progressives want the Church to rely on witness and persuasion to spread its teaching; they want more collegial models of authority and an erasure of the hierarchical distinctions that, for example, make women ineligible to be priests; and they want the Church to be more open to learning from non-Catholics even if it must rethink traditional dogmas as a result. But traditionalists want to cooperate with political power to enforce Catholic teaching—for example, on abortion; they want to strengthen and re-centralize hierarchical authority; they want to enforce strict and clear standards of orthodoxy.

There is much in the teaching of Pope John Paul II that would encourage this traditionalist interpretation. In the theology of John Paul II—a theology deeply influenced by his experiences in his native Poland, where Catholicism and nationalism have been closely identified—civil society is regarded with some suspicion. The Church is seen as the public guardian of an objective moral order—an order that should not tolerate private groups (for instance, abortion-rights groups) whose aims and purposes are contrary to orthodox Catholic faith and morals. "Democracy," the pope warns in his encyclical "The Gospel of Life," "cannot be idolized to the point of making it a substitute for morality or a panacea for immorality. . . . Its moral value is not automatic, but depends on conformity to the moral law to which it, like every other form of human behavior, must be subject." [27]

As we have seen, the theology of the Chinese Catholic Church is closer to Pope John Paul II's vision than to the visions common in the United States, where most Catholics (to the exasperation of the pope) accept the pluralism of society and take for granted the need to separate church and state. Indeed, the Chinese Catholic Church was formed by a pre-Vatican II, Counter Reformation theology that was even more authoritarian and less tolerant of moral pluralism than the pope's.

Around the world, the traditionalists seem to be gaining strength, not just because Pope John Paul II leans to their side but because they often have more singleness of purpose and access to more money than the progressives do. In the United States, at least, the traditionalists provide most of the support for the underground Church. They are able to raise far more money for this work than organizations seeking liaison with the official Church. But because of the beleaguered context in which

Chinese Catholics live, when the serious divisions among U.S. Catholics are imported to China, they can lead to potentially catastrophic divisions among Chinese Catholics.

One way to help Chinese Catholics avoid such divisions would be to improve the political climate. The belligerence and truculence that characterize some Catholic communities (along with many other Chinese communities) is indeed the legacy not just of traditional particularism and factionalism but of the harshness of Communist Party rule. As we have seen, besides nourishing the flower of faith, martyrdom also produces the thorns of division. It raises the heat in discussions about who is a worthy member of the community. It tempts the community to self-righteousness and even to revenge. The government has itself to blame for the suspiciousness and fractiousness of its citizens. If it tries to suppress threats to its rule with force, in the long run the problems will become more virulent than ever. The Chinese government needs encouragement and prodding to reform itself in a way that inspires true popular respect rather than maintaining itself in power through despotic force.

If the government were willing and able to undertake such reforms, the Vatican might help to improve the political climate for Chinese Catholics by normalizing diplomatic relations with China and negotiating compromises that would give the Chinese government a strong, legitimate voice in the appointment of bishops. (A model for the naming of bishops could be that followed by the Church in Vietnam, where the Vatican and the government must reach agreement on appointment of bishops.) There are a number of obstacles in the way of normalizing relations: for example, the People's Republic's demands that the Vatican sever its diplomatic relations with Taiwan and the Vatican's concern not to offend clergy and laity who have suffered martyrdom for resisting the Chinese government. Most of the obstacles could probably be overcome, though, if the will to normalize existed on both sides. Perhaps this normalization will not occur until more liberal-minded successors to both Pope John Paul II and Deng Xiaoping are firmly in place.[28]

While political normalization would alleviate the ambiguities about legitimate authority that so deeply confuse and divide the Chinese Church and would probably lead to a lessening of the political harassment that instills hatred and paranoia within the Catholic community, it would not eliminate the social causes of division and conflict. The tension between a rural, folk piety and an urban, reflexive faith would still exist. There would be tensions between those who want to wall themselves into a localized world of God and those who seek an open, cosmopolitan faith. Such tensions would exist because they permeate all of Chinese society and culture. It should be clear that my sympathies lie with the open, cosmopolitan culture of the city, and my hope is that an emerging urban middle class will eventually give rise to a vigorous, pluralistic civil society. But in a society that is still 70 percent rural and marked by deep regional differences and widening disparities of wealth—and is still haunted by collective memories of violence and repression—it will be at least another generation before a secure, self-confident middle class emerges. Whether that middle class will have any sense of transcendent meaning, any commitment to social responsibility, and any of those habits of moral discipline that would enable it to develop a democratic civic culture will depend on the vitality of Chinese institutions for moral education. The Chinese Catholic Church, at best, could make only a small contribution to this moral education, and it could make that contribution only if it reformed itself. But there may be analogies between the difficulties and opportunities faced by the Catholic Church and the difficulties and opportunities faced by other Chinese institutions of moral education—including the Communist Party—as they undergo moral reform in a new China.

THE CATHOLIC CHURCH IN GREATER CHINA

Relevant models of reform might be found in Hong Kong and Taiwan. In these places, a large, vocal middle class and a lively civil society have emerged. Though small (about 5 percent of the population in Hong Kong and only around 1.5 percent in Taiwan), the Catholic Church has played an important role in morally educating these civil societies.[29]

In Hong Kong, the Church runs many elementary and secondary schools (including such prestigious high schools as the Maryknoll Convent School), hospitals, social-welfare organizations, even a news service, as well as innumerable social clubs, youth groups, women's associations, workers' centers, and social-advocacy groups. Although priests and sisters usually play important and sometimes key roles in such organizations and associations, laypeople play active and often dominant parts. Like much of the rest of Hong Kong's civil society, many Catholic organizations, especially the schools, hospitals, and social-welfare organizations, were heavily subsidized by the British colonial government. Indeed, that government long relied on all sorts of nongovernmental organizations, prominently including religious organizations, to deliver educational and social-welfare services. To receive government services, such groups, including the Catholic Church, had to become increasingly professionalized in their management and style of service delivery and had to work cooperatively with people of all religious and secular backgrounds. Their leadership was also by and large co-opted by the government. They became "service providers" rather than "advocates." On the margins of the Catholic Church, however, networks of "progressive Catholics," consisting mostly of relatively young priests and sisters, idealistic lay intellectuals, and some workers, have taken an active role in pushing for social justice—advocating more generous social-welfare benefits from the government and better wages and working conditions from corporations. Though not especially encouraged by Hong Kong's prelate, Cardinal John Wu, and by most senior clergy, these progressive Catholics—who often work ecumenically with Protestants and secular activists—have been a vocal presence in Hong Kong society and have had some influence in putting social justice on the public agenda. Finally, some of the most prominent Democratic Party members in the legislative council that was elected in 1994 but disbanded when Hong Kong reverted to Chinese rule in 1997 were Catholic laypeople—the most well known is the chairman, Martin Lee—who explicitly credit their Catholic education with giving them their sense of social responsibility.

Many Hong Kong Catholics have been concerned about how the Church will in the long run be treated under Chinese sovereignty. Precisely because it is a moral force within Hong Kong's civil society, the Catholic Church seems problematic to the People's Republic of China. Though promising to maintain Hong Kong's social system for at least fifty years, the Chinese authorities may be unsympathetic to the social movements occasionally stirred up by networks of progressive Catholics. Insofar as advocates of democracy like Martin Lee get some of their motivation from their Catholic education, this influence too may be problematic. Finally, within the Hong Kong Catholic Church there are partisans of both the official Church and the underground Church in China; and indeed Hong Kong Catholics have been major sources of funds for some parts of the underground Church, as well as major sources of information about human-rights abuses against the underground. The potential certainly exists for conflict between Hong Kong Catholics and their new government. However, skillful Church leadership may help to avoid conflict. Cardinal Wu has been playing a crucial diplomatic role in trying to reconcile the Church in mainland China with the Vatican. At the end of 1996, the pope appointed two new bishops in Hong Kong, one of whom, John Tong, has long worked at the Holy Spirit Study Centre and been active in building bridges with the mainland Church. Perhaps in the end the Hong Kong Church will influence the religious and even the civil climate in the mainland more than it is influenced by the policy of the People's Republic.

In Taiwan, the Catholic Church has played much less of a role in primary and secondary education than in Hong Kong, but it runs highly regarded Fu Jen University. Catholics have also helped to organize a wide variety of associations, from rural credit cooperatives to workers' associations to aborigine support groups to student associations. The Church has made important contributions to health and social welfare and has taken the lead in extending compassionate care to people like the mentally handicapped who have often been ignored in Chinese society. Catholic theologians and social scientists from Fu Jen University have put forth important ideas about how to adapt Catholic theology to Confucian culture and how to apply Catholic moral teachings to the problems raised by Taiwan's rapidly developing society.

However, the Catholic Church in Taiwan seemed to stagnate once a vigorous civil society sprang up in the 1980s. Already small, the number of practicing Catholics is declining. Although the liturgy was beautifully celebrated and the sermon intelligently thoughtful, the chapel at Fu Jen University was only about half full for Sunday Mass when I visited there, and my priest friends told me that this attendance was typical. (However, the chapel was packed for a Mass in Tagalog for Filipino workers employed in that part of Taiwan.)

Catholics in Taiwan have many explanations for the decline. One is that most of the bishops and clergy of Taiwan were displaced mainlanders who never made a serious effort to build the Church among the 80 percent of the population who are native Taiwanese. Another is that the Church did not do enough to encourage the initiative of its laity, partly because until the 1980s the Church could rely heavily on money and personnel from abroad. Still another is that the Church simply could not develop its teachings fast enough to keep pace with a society that has undergone such rapid economic and political development over the past generation.[30]

While the Church, for whatever reasons, has been declining, Taiwan's secular civil society has been flourishing. Since the mid-1980s—especially since the ending of martial law in 1987—thousands of private voluntary associations have sprung up: research organizations, philanthropies, social-service organizations, community-improvement associations, along with a large number of social-advocacy groups promoting environmental protection, women's concerns, aborigine rights, and a host of other causes. Some of the secular advocacy groups are picking up issues that in earlier times were raised by Christian missionaries. For instance, the Garden of Hope Foundation, founded by a crusading journalist, tries to raise awareness about child prostitution and provides a shelter for girls wishing to escape the brothels. Shelters run by Catholic missionaries in the 1960s tried to do the same thing (without unfortunately making a major dent in the number of child prostitutes).[31]

Among the philanthropies and social-service organizations, the most popular are based on Chinese religions, Buddhism and Daoism, but influenced by Catholic and Protestant patterns of social activism. The most popular philanthropic organization in Taiwan is the Tsu-chi Foundation, established by a charismatic Buddhist nun. Dubbed the "Mother Theresa of Asia," the nun Master Cheng Yen claims that she got the idea for her work from Catholic missionary nuns in her home city of Hualien. Now her charitable foundation, skillfully managed by professionals, draws in over two hundred million dollars a year and runs hospitals, a medical school, and various programs to alleviate poverty.[32] Also Daoist temples, like the Hsin Tien Kung Temple in Taipei, have developed similar educational, medical, and social-service programs. These programs cooperate with and reach out to people of all faiths, not just to practicing Buddhists or Daoists. It is as if the model of social engagement promoted by the Catholic Church, especially since Vatican II, has flourished after having been grafted onto religious traditions with deeper roots in Taiwanese soil. The Catholic Church thus may have had a significant moral influence on the development of Taiwan's civil society even though it has been losing its institutional strength.

Taiwan's flourishing civil society renders problematic any plan for reunification with the mainland. This problem arises only partly because some of the newly active groups are carriers of Taiwanese nationalism. It arises also because the groups foster a range and a variety of civic initiatives that would make it difficult for the mainland government (assuming it retains its present form) to control Taiwan's society. Attempts by the People's Republic to subdue such groups would probably result in a messy negative counterreaction. Alternatively, the rulers on the mainland might be impressed by how dynamic and prosperous Taiwan's civil society is and might appreciate the role played by religious groups in inspiring and imparting moral substance to that civil society—and consequently might want to emulate it. It remains to be seen whether Hong Kong and Taiwan will "convert" the People's Republic or whether it will be the other way around.

THE WORLD OF GOD AND THE KINGDOM OF GOD

What kind of conversion should a Christian hope for? No Christian would want the corrupt tyranny of the Chinese Communist Party extended. Yet Christians are also challenged to resist the rampant materialism and consumerism of present-day Hong Kong and Taiwan. A priest in Taiwan reports that he recently officiated at a wedding that the groom interrupted three times in order to take calls on his wireless phone. (The parish has now made a rule—no phone conversations during your wedding ceremony.) Is a Catholic community that has been so invaded by consumer culture able to sustain the spiritual commitment that the Church says should be the foundation of marriage?

The Church in mainland China presents an alternative vision, a vision of a Church-dominated world of God that takes two different forms centered around two different images of Christ. On Sunday morning at St. Joseph's Cathedral in Tianjin there is a splendid solemn high Mass, said in Latin with all the glorious pomp of the Counter Reformation liturgy. After the Mass is finished, the people file out, and the brilliant candles on the altar and all the lights in the church are extinguished. Then members of the underground Church file in. In the dim light, led by a man dressed in ordinary street clothes, they say the Stations of the Cross. The first congregation worships Christ the King, triumphant over the world, who established a Church that would enfold all the material and spiritual riches of this world and the next. The second congregation worships Christ Crucified, the suffering servant, despised and rejected, who through his agony redeems the world.

The resurrected Christ of Catholic tradition is of course at once both king and suffering servant, which makes no sense in human terms but to people of faith represents the power and wisdom of God. To emphasize one image at the expense of the other is to distort the Christian faith. The Church that would make itself in the image of Christ the King attempts to dominate the world with the help of worldly powers in the hope of producing here on earth an ecclesiastical world of God that reflects the glory of God in heaven. The Church that would make itself exclusively in the image of the suffering servant walls itself off from the joys and comforts of the outside world and forms a resentment-filled, ghettoized world of God.

The challenge to the Church that would be a sign of grace to the civil societies struggling to be born and struggling to survive at the end of the twentieth century is to represent in its symbols and deeds the tension between the two images of Christ. Maintaining this tension entails giving up the notion of creating a world of God here on earth. In open, pluralistic societies, the Church does not have the resources effectively to utilize political, economic, or even social pressure to enforce a monopoly of meaning in the world. Insofar as the Church wants to affirm the emergence of such societies, it has to take seriously Jesus's statement to Pilate, "My kingdom is not of this world."

Yet it also has to take seriously a traditional Christian injunction, affirmed by twentieth-century papal encyclicals, to cherish the world as God's creation and to work within the world so as to improve it, to make it more just, less selfish, more devoted to the common good. In a pluralistic society, the Church has to present its message through education and persuasion. In a complex, postindustrial, knowledge- and information-based society, that education cannot be based on an authoritarian pedagogy in which a dogmatic vision is imparted to ignorant pupils. As Julio de Santa Ana, a Protestant theologian with the World Council of Churches, puts it, "The Roman Catholic Church calls itself 'mater et magistra.' If it is 'magistra,' then it is difficult to sit around the same table, on the same foot of equality with other members of civil society. . . . The church can teach lessons to the people but not live with associations of the people on the same level." [33] A civil society is a world governed by no comprehensive system, a world formed by the contingent conjunction of many different parts. Many people find civil society refreshing and hopeful because it is a world without dogmas, a world constantly open to new possibilities. In a civil society, the Church has to be a teacher that educates through dialogue, through being attentive to the ever changing signs of the times.

In China, and indeed throughout the world, such a task requires not just a revivified Church but a resurrected one—a Church transformed and renewed. Such a Church would have vitally important good news to proclaim. Through biblical word and sacrament, it would carry on the memory of its suffering servant founder. It would proclaim that in the depth of life are goods infinitely more important than worldly wealth, status, and power. It would give sinful, estranged, and fearful people everywhere a hope that they are part of a story that will end in love and forgiveness and redemption. The sacrifices of the Chinese Church's many heroic martyrs and the daily devotion of its many ordinary believers bear witness to this hope. Watching the signs of the times, a Church that dares to continually reform itself may make that hope present not just in China but in the United States and in modern worlds everywhere groaning for reform.

Notes

INTRODUCTION: THE CONTEXT
OF CHINESE CATHOLICISM

1. Subsequently, urban enterprises changed to a five-day workweek.

2. This scene was also described in Richard Madsen, "The Catholic Church in China Today: A New Rites Controversy?" in *The Chinese Rites Controversy: Its History and Meaning*, ed. D. E. Mungello (Sankt Augustin, Germany: Institut Monumenta Serica, 1994), pp. 267–269.

3. Official government statistics and Church-produced statistics on the number of Catholics vary widely. The Chinese Catholic Patriotic Association, which is under government control, says that there are only about 3.8 million Catholics. In one of its reports, the state statistical bureau said there are 12 million. In my judgment, the best estimates of the Catholic population are by the Hong Kong Catholic sociologist Anthony Lam, who puts the number at 10 million. This figure is based on an analysis independent of that of the state statistical bureau. It sums up figures given in the reports of local dioceses, and it takes into account peasants' failures to register births in excess of those allowed by the one-child policy and their reluctance to enter their names in official parish registers. Anthony Lam, "How Many Catholics Are There in China?" *Tripod* 71 (September–October 1992): 51–57. (*Tripod* is published by the Holy Spirit Study Centre in Hong Kong.)

According to Jean Charbonnier, *Guide to the Catholic Church in China* (Singapore: China Catholic Communication, 1997), there are 138 dioceses, 73 government-approved bishops and perhaps 62 underground bishops, about 1,500 priests (over half ordained since 1985), about 2,000 sisters (most of them young), and 5,000 officially approved churches and chapels.

4. Some representative social science books in English are C. K. Yang, *Religion in Chinese Society* (Berkeley: University of California Press, 1961); Richard C. Bush, Jr., *Religion in Communist China* (Nashville, Tenn.: Abingdon Press, 1970); Donald E. MacInnis, *Religious Policy and Practice in Communist China* (New York: Macmillan, 1972); Daniel L. Overmeyer, *Religions of China* (New York: Harper & Row, 1986); Donald E. MacInnis, *Religion in China Today: Policy and Practice* (Maryknoll, N.Y.: Orbis Books, 1989); Luo Zhufeng, ed., *Religion under Socialist China* (Zhongguo shehui zhuyi shiqide zhongjiao wenti), trans. Donald E. MacInnis and Zheng Xi'an (Armonk, N.Y.: Sharpe, 1991); Eric O. Hanson, *Catholic Politics in China and Korea* (Maryknoll, N.Y.: Orbis Books, 1980); Laszlo Ladany, *The Catholic Church in China* (New York: Freedom House, 1987); Kim-kwong Chan, *Towards a Contextual Ecclesiology: The Catholic Church in the People's Republic of China (1979–1983): Its Life and Theological Implications* (Hong Kong: Photech Systems, 1987); Alan Hunter and Kim-kwong Chan, *Protestantism in Contemporary China* (Cambridge: Cambridge University Press, 1993); Dru C. Gladney, *Muslim Chinese: Ethnic Nationalism in the People's Republic* (Cambridge, Mass.: Harvard University Council on East Asian Studies, 1991).

5. This pamphlet was dated "Feast of Pentecost, 1993." This and all translations of Chinese materials, except for those otherwise attributed, are mine.

6. Vaclav Havel, "Remarks upon Receiving the Philadelphia Liberty Medal in Independence Hall, July 4, 1994," in *The Art of the Impossible: Politics as Morality and Practice: Speeches and Writings, 1990–1996* (New York: Knopf, 1997), p. 166.

7. The May Fourth Movement is the name given to the period of iconoclastic cultural criticism that lasted from about 1914 to 1924. The name comes from the student demonstrations that took place on May 4, 1919, in response to the publication of the Versailles Peace Treaty, which transferred Germany's Chinese concessions to Japan rather than back to China.

8. Jiwei Ci, *Dialectic of the Chinese Revolution: From Utopianism to Hedonism* (Stanford, Calif.: Stanford University Press, 1994), p. 115.

9. Su Xiaokang, "My Views on a 'Sense of Mission,'" *Qiu Shi* 2 (1988): 47–48; translated in Su Xiaokang and Wang Luxiang, *Deathsong of the River: A Reader's Guide to the Chinese TV Series Heshang*, trans. and ed. Richard W. Bodman and Pin P. Wan (Ithaca, N.Y.: Cornell University East Asia Program, 1991), pp. 42–43.

10. For a good summary of the main approaches to the anthropology and sociology of religion, see T. M. Luhrmann, "The Ugly Goddess: Reflections on the Role of Violent Images in Religious Experience," unpublished paper, University of California, San Diego, 1996.

11. Representative theoretical works include Ernest Gellner, *Conditions of Liberty: Civil Society and Its Rivals* (New York: Penguin Books, 1994); John Keane, *Democracy and Civil Society* (New York: Verso, 1988); Jean Cohen and Andrew Arato, *Civil Society and Political Theory* (Cambridge, Mass.: MIT Press, 1992); Charles Taylor, "Modes of Civil Society," *Public Culture* 3, no. 1 (Fall 1990): 95–131; Michael Walzer, "The Idea of Civil Society," *Dissent* 38, no. 2 (Spring 1991): 293–304. A good summary of the civil-society debate as

applied to China is in the special issue of *Modern China* devoted to that topic: *Modern China* 19, no. 2 (April 1993). For empirical detail, see Tadashi Yamamoto, *Emerging Civil Society in the Asia Pacific Community: Nongovernmental Underpinnings of the Emerging Asia Pacific Regional Community* (Singapore and Tokyo: Institute of Southeast Asian Studies and Japan Centre for International Exchange, 1995).

    12. Gellner, *Conditions of Liberty*.

    13. William M. Sullivan, "The Infrastructure of Democracy: From Civil Society to Civic Community," unpublished paper, La Salle University, n.d., p. 1.

    14. See Robert N. Bellah et al., "The House Divided: Introduction to the Updated Edition," in *Habits of the Heart: Individualism and Commitment in American Life*, rev. ed. (Berkeley: University of California Press, 1996).

    15. In my view, much of the recent debate in the United States about whether a decline in the number of private voluntary associations is an indicator of the decline in the capacity of citizens for democratic self-governance is confused by the fact that the debate is carried out in quantitative terms without regard for the quality of the groups being counted as presumed parts of civil society. The debate centers around Robert D. Putnam's articles "Bowling Alone: America's Declining Social Capital," *Journal of Democracy* 6, no. 1 (January 1995): 65–78, and "The Strange Disappearance of Civil America," *American Prospect* 24 (Winter 1996): 34–48. See also Michael Schudson, "What If Civic Life Didn't Die?" (17–25), Theda Skocpol, "Unravelling from Above" (20–25), and Richard M. Vallely, "Couch-Potato Democracy?" (25–26), all in *American Prospect* 25 (March–April 1996); and William A. Galston, "Won't You Be My Neighbor?" (16–18), Alejandro Portes and Patricia Landolt, "The Downside of Social Capital" (16–21), both in *American Prospect* 26 (May–June 1996). My response is in Richard Madsen, "Community, Civil Society, and Social Ecology," in *Report from Euro-American Workshop* (forthcoming).

    16. *Washington Post*, 4 June 1996, p. A1.

    17. Publications include Yanjie Bian and John R. Logan, "Market Transition and the Persistence of Power: The Changing Stratification System in Urban China," *American Sociological Review* 61, no. 5 (October 1996): 739–758; D. Ruan et al., "Suppose You Gave a Survey and Everybody Came," *Cultural Anthropology Methods* 6: 12; D. Ruan et al., "On the Changing Structure of Social Networks in Urban China," *Social Networks* 19: 75–89; L. C. Freeman and D. Ruan, "An International Comparative Study of Interpersonal Behavior and Role Relationships," *L'Année Sociologique* 47: 89–115. As yet unpublished papers include Christopher Earle Nevitt, "Private Business Associations in China: Civil Society or Tools of Local Government Autonomy?"; David K. Jordan, "Tianjin Matchmaking"; Brett Sheehan, "Elite Mobilization in Early Twentieth Century Tianjin"; Li Baoliang, "The Private Sector as a Social Stratum"; Zhang Wenhong, "Discussion Networks in Urban Tianjin"; Pan Yunkang, "The Family Network in China—The Transition from Traditional Family to Urban Family"; Wang Hui, "Evolving Civil Society in Tianjin"; Li Shiyu, "Tianjin Culture." (The unpublished papers are available through the Sociology Department, University of California, San Diego.)

    18. X. L. Ding, "Institutional Amphibiousness and the Transition from

Communism: The Case of China," *British Journal of Political Science* 24, pt. 3 (July 1994): 293–317; and X. L. Ding, *The Decline of Communism in China: Legitimacy Crisis, 1977–1989* (Cambridge: Cambridge University Press, 1994), p. 26.

19. Robert D. Putnam, *Making Democracy Work: Civic Traditions in Modern Italy* (Princeton, N.J.: Princeton University Press, 1993), pp. 87–90.

20. Holy Spirit Study Centre, Hong Kong; China Catholic Communication, Singapore; Relais France-Chine, Paris; Ferdinand Verbiest Foundation, Leuven, Belgium; China-Zentrum, Sankt Augustin, Germany; Amitie-Chine, Montreal; Cardinal Kung Foundation, Stamford, Connecticut; U.S. Catholic China Bureau, Orange, New Jersey.

21. For example, *Family News of the Catholic Church in China* (Hong Kong: Holy Spirit Study Centre, 1990); *Spring Rain* (Hong Kong: Holy Spirit Study Centre, 1990); Rik De Gendt, *A New Life for the Church in China* (Manila: Bookmark, 1990). See also the video *Living Temples,* produced by the Kuangch'i Program Service, Taipei, 1991.

22. Most important articles on religion from the Chinese press and scholarly journals are translated into English in the *China Study Journal,* published in London by the Council of Churches of Britain and Ireland.

23. Eriberto P. Lozada, Jr., is completing fieldwork for a dissertation on Catholic villages in Guangdong Province; these communities do not have the conflicts that are so obvious in some other regions (personal communication).

24. See Shi Guoming et al., "Sunan diqu yumin xinyang tianzhujiao wenti chutan" (Preliminary study of Catholic fishermen in the Sunan area), *Zongjiao* 6 (November 1984): 36–42.

25. According to a report cited in *The New Republic,* 7 July 1997, "The police destroyed 15,000 religious sites in Zhejiang province alone in 1996. In January [1996], Father Guo Bo Le of Shanghai was sentenced to two years of re-education, according to the court decision, for 'saying Mass.' In March, during Holy Week, public security officials raided the home of the bishop of Shanghai and confiscated numerous religious texts" (22).

CHAPTER 1. HIERARCHY AND HISTORY: THE PROBLEM OF AUTHORITY IN THE CHINESE CATHOLIC CHURCH

1. The Kangxi emperor's edict defined Catholicism—at least the kind of Catholicism being taught by the Jesuits—as consistent with orthodox Confucian learning. Soon after the emperor's edict, the pope declared that the accommodations made by the Jesuits to Chinese culture were unacceptable, which led the Chinese emperor to ban Catholicism.

2. My view of the logic of hierarchy is based on Louis Dumont, *Homo Hierarchicus: An Essay on the Caste System,* trans. Mark Sainsbury (Chicago: University of Chicago Press, 1970).

3. Second Vatican Council, *Lumen Gentium* (Dogmatic constitution on the Church) (Washington, D.C.: United States Catholic Conference of Publishing and Promotion Services, 1964).

4. There is a vast literature on the Rites Controversy. Some of the most important English books are George H. Dunne, S.J., *Generation of Giants: The Story of the Jesuits in China in the Last Decades of the Ming Dynasty* (Notre Dame, Ind.: University of Notre Dame Press, 1962); George Minamiki, S.J., *The Chinese Rites Controversy: From Its Beginnings to Modern Times* (Chicago: Loyola University Press, 1985); Donald F. St. Sure, S.J., trans., *100 Roman Documents concerning the Chinese Rites Controversy (1645–1941)* (San Francisco: Ricci Institute, University of San Francisco, 1992); J. S. Cummins, *A Question of Rites: Friar Domingo Navarrete and the Jesuits in China* (Aldershot, Hants.: Scolar, 1993); D. E. Mungello, ed., *The Chinese Rites Controversy: Its History and Meaning* (Sankt Augustin, Germany: Monumenta Serica, 1994); and Andrew C. Ross, *A Vision Betrayed: The Jesuits in Japan and China, 1542–1742* (Maryknoll, N.Y.: Orbis Books, 1994).

5. The papal decree of 1704 was reaffirmed and strengthened by Clement XI's 1715 apostolic constitution *Ex illa die;* finally, in 1742 Pope Benedict XIV issued the decree *Ex quo singulari,* which not only confirmed Clement XI's decision but prohibited any further discussion of the matter. See St. Sure, *100 Roman Documents,* pp. 41, 47–62.

6. The best summaries of this phase of missionary history include Paul A. Cohen, *China and Christianity: The Missionary Movement and the Growth of Chinese Antiforeignism, 1860–1870* (Ann Arbor: University of Michigan Press, 1963); Kenneth Scott Latourette, *A History of Christian Missions in China* (New York: Macmillan, 1929); and Columba Cary-Elwes, *China and the Cross: A Survey of Missionary History* (New York: P. J. Kennedy and Sons, 1957). See also Hanson, *Catholic Politics in China and Korea,* pp. 15–31; Joseph W. Esherick, *The Origins of the Boxer Uprising* (Berkeley: University of California Press, 1987), pp. 68–95; and Ernest P. Young, "The Politics of Evangelism at the End of the Qing: Nanchang, 1906," in *Christianity in China: From the Eighteenth Century to the Present,* ed. Daniel H. Bays (Stanford, Calif.: Stanford University Press, 1996), pp. 91–113.

7. See Esherick, *Origins of the Boxer Uprising.*

8. The political context for these events is summarized in Jean-Paul Wiest, *Maryknoll in China* (Armonk, N.Y.: Sharpe, 1988), pp. 45–47; and Hanson, *Catholic Politics in China and Korea,* pp. 20–26. The text of *Maximum Illud* is given in Minamiki, *The Chinese Rites Controversy,* p. 190.

9. Kim-kwong Chan, *Struggling for Survival: The Catholic Church in China from 1949–1970* (Hong Kong: Christian Study Centre on Religion and Culture, 1992), pp. 8–10.

10. Richard Madsen, *Morality and Power in a Chinese Village* (Berkeley: University of California Press, 1994); and Yang, *Religion in Chinese Society,* pp. 378–404.

11. Hanson, *Catholic Politics in China and Korea,* pp. 87–88, 92–93.

12. Chan, *Struggling for Survival,* pp. 22–23. Founded in Dublin in 1922, the Legion of Mary was supposed to carry out spiritual "warfare . . . against the world and its evil power." *The Official Handbook of the Legion of Mary* (Louisville, Ky.: Publishers Printing, 1953). The Chinese translation of the name

of the Legion is the "Army" of Mary. For an account of the Legion of Mary that reflects its assertive anti-Communist efforts, see G. Palmer, *God's Underground in Asia* (New York: Appleton-Century-Crofts, 1953).

13. Chan, *Struggling for Survival*, pp. 22–23.

14. Ibid., p. 23.

15. A few fared worse. Bishop Francis Ford of Maryknoll died of exhaustion and illness in a Chinese prison in 1952; and Bishop James E. Walsh, who stayed in China long after other missionaries had left, was imprisoned in 1958 and released only in 1970. Wiest, *Maryknoll in China*, pp. 400–403.

16. James Townsend, *Political Participation in Communist China* (Berkeley: University of California Press, 1967).

17. Chan, *Struggling for Survival*, pp. 29–31. Also, John Tong, "The Church from 1949 to 1990," in *The Catholic Church in Modern China*, ed. Edmond Tang and Jean-Paul Wiest (Maryknoll, N.Y.: Orbis Books, 1993), pp. 8–11. The papal encyclical was entitled *Cupimus Imprimis*.

18. Chan, *Struggling for Survival*, pp. 37–45. Tong, "The Church from 1949 to 1990," pp. 11–12. Hanson, *Catholic Politics in China and Korea*, pp. 72–82.

19. Chan, *Struggling for Survival*, pp. 50–58. Tong, "The Church from 1949 to 1990," pp. 10–15.

20. For a summary of the relevant provisions of canon law, see Chan, *Towards a Contextual Ecclesiology*, pp. 250–253.

21. We often heard accounts of such practices during our interviews.

22. An English translation of this document is in MacInnis, *Religion in China Today*, pp. 8–26.

23. In the late 1970s, the National Catholic Administrative Committee was established to complement the work of the Chinese Catholic Patriotic Association. The functions and the personnel of these two groups closely overlap. The "two committees," as Catholics refer to these agencies of ecclesiastical control, in effect function as one committee.

24. Chan, *Towards a Contextual Ecclesiology*, pp. 278–314. Beatrice Leung, *Sino-Vatican Relations: Problems in Conflicting Authority, 1976–1986* (Cambridge: Cambridge University Press, 1992), pp. 189–231.

25. Catholics in the United States dispute which names to use for the groups that I have called the "public Church" (or sometimes the "official Church") and the "underground Church." The newsletter of the Cardinal Kung Foundation, which is a partisan of the underground Church, refers to the underground as simply the "Roman Catholic Church in China," and it refers to the public Church as the "Chinese Catholic Patriotic Association" and claims it is a false Church. The United States Catholic China Bureau, which is sympathetic to the public Church, uses the public Church/underground Church terminology. It argues that Catholics who worship in public in venues approved of by the government do not necessarily identify themselves with or even belong to the Patriotic Association. They should therefore be considered the part of the one Catholic Church that has arranged to practice its faith publicly under government regulations, while the underground Church should be considered the part that practices its faith in violation of government regulations. Thus there is only one Church, although it is obviously divided into various factions. In using the

terms *public* or *official Church,* on the one hand, and *underground Church* on the other, I am not arguing that all factions are indeed truly Catholic. That is for Church authorities—and God—to decide. I am simply withholding judgment on this religious issue while acknowledging that all parties claim to be truly Catholic.

26. Details learned from interviews in 1994.

27. These figures were published in the London Catholic newspaper *The Tablet* in 1994. People familiar with the situation are reluctant to provide the latest figures for fear of endangering some of the Vatican-approved bishops in China.

28. Latin text is provided in Chan, *Towards a Contextual Ecclesiology,* pp. 438–442.

29. Edmond Tang, "The Church into the 1990s," in *The Catholic Church in Modern China,* ed. Edmond Tang and John-Paul Wiest (Maryknoll, N.Y.: Orbis Books, 1993), pp. 32–35.

30. The government published several documents in the early 1990s specifying the new harder line. The first of these was Communist Party "Document 6," published in 1991, which was presented as a supplement to the 1982 Document 19. Document 6 emphasized the need to prevent "unlawful activities and infiltration from abroad" and tightened the procedures for approving new religious venues. In 1994, the State Council issued two decrees—"Decrees 144 and 145"—aimed at implementing the policies specified in Document 6.

31. Among many depressing examples: Asia Watch, *Continuing Religious Repression in China* (New York: Asia Watch, 1993) (arrests of priests and nuns, harassment of Catholic laity, the suspicious death of Bishop Fan Xueyan); Amnesty International, *Report,* March 1995 (arbitrary detention of, torture of— hanging upside down, electric shocks to the mouth—and fines against Catholics who have violated birth-control policies); Amnesty International, *Urgent Action* (New York: Amnesty International, 1995) (rearrest of seventy-six-year-old Bishop Zeng Jingmu, who was suffering from pneumonia after a stint in prison that ended one month previously); *China Focus,* November 1996 (new wave of persecution against Catholics in the Baoding region of Hebei Province; Catholics forbidden to leave village without permission from authorities; priests arrested; Catholic students expelled from school unless they denounced their religion; nuns subjected to sexual harassment); Patrick E. Tyler, "Catholics in China: Back to the Underground," *New York Times,* 26 January 1997, p. 1 (in a raid carried out by "thousands of paramilitary police supported by armored car units and helicopters," Marian shrine at Donglu destroyed, statue of Virgin Mary confiscated, two bishops arrested).

32. Some of the pictures were printed in *Zhonglian,* the Singapore Catholic journal, in 1993.

33. Asia Watch, *Continuing Religious Repression in China,* pp. 10–11.

34. See the documents related to the underground Church published in Edmond Tang and Jean-Paul Wiest, eds., *The Catholic Church in Modern China* (Maryknoll, N.Y.: Orbis Books, 1993), pp. 120–152.

35. "China Church Update," *Tripod* 71 (September–October 1992): 58.

36. The French missionaries who developed the Church throughout East

Asia in the late nineteenth century often practiced a cult of martyrdom. An example is the legend of Blessed Theophane Venard, who "decided at the age of nine that he would go to Indochina as a priest and die for God." Ordained a priest of MEP, he was sent to Indochina, where he was beheaded during an anti-Catholic persecution in 1900. According to the legend, his executioner "had promised a swift, thorough execution in exchange for Father Venard's clothes. The priest replied softly, 'The longer it lasts, the better it will be.' He went joyfully to his death with the words 'Jesus, Mary, and Joseph' on his lips." Ray Harrison, *Bishop Walsh of Maryknoll: Prisoner of Red China* (New York: Putnam, 1962), pp. 44–45. For the Chinese spirit of revolutionary asceticism, see Madsen, *Morality and Power in a Chinese Village*.

37. UCAN News, August 11, 1992. The murderer was tried and executed. He may have been deranged, and there is no evidence that his actions were deliberately planned or approved by any Catholic group. But the atmosphere of hostility in the Catholic Church was probably conducive to this crime.

38. UCAN News, January 20, 1994: "underground Catholics attend church built by government approved Church."

39. Ding, *The Decline of Communism in China*, p. 26.

CHAPTER 2. COMMUNITY AND SOLIDARITY

1. Quoted in Wiest, *Maryknoll in China*, p. 76.

2. There are no precise statistics on the distribution of Catholics. About 75 percent of China's population lives in rural areas, however, and rural people are clearly overrepresented in the Catholic Church. According to statistics furnished by the Bishop of Tianjin, for example, about 80 percent of the Catholics in that municipality come not from the city proper but from the rural suburbs under the jurisdiction of the municipality. Moreover, the vast majority of China's 113 dioceses are centered not in large municipalities but in small provincial cities. And the largest Catholic concentrations in China are in rural districts like Xian County in Hebei. "An Accurate and Truthful Survey Report: Assessment of 'Present Situation of and Reflections on the Catholic Church in Villages around Tianjin,' " *China Study Journal* 6, no. 3 (1991): 45–48.

3. Owen Lattimore, *High Tartary* (1930; reprint, New York: Kodansha International, 1994), p. 49.

4. For a careful analysis of how the Church integrated social, economic, and cultural structures in the nineteenth century and how this integration put local Catholic communities at odds with non-Catholics, see Charles A. Litzinger, "Rural Religion and Village Organization in North China: The Catholic Challenge in the Late Nineteenth Century," and Roger R. Thompson, "Twilight of the Gods in the Chinese Countryside: Christians, Confucians, and the Modernizing State, 1861–1911," both in *Christianity in China: From the Eighteenth Century to the Present*, ed. Daniel H. Bays (Stanford, Calif.: Stanford University Press, 1996), pp. 41–52 and 53–72. For community-building practice in the early twentieth century, see Wiest, *Maryknoll in China*, pp. 119–120: "Maryknollers viewed their missionary role in China as two-fold: the first step was to make converts and baptize well-defined social units such as a family, clan, or

village, rather than individuals with no group support. Equally important was the second step of organizing the new Catholics into faithful parishes which would radiate Christian life into the surrounding villages and towns."

5. This is especially true, perhaps, in northern China. In southern coastal areas, like Fujian and Guangdong, there is a great deal of new temple building, often accomplished with money from Overseas Chinese.

6. "Selected Reports on Investigations of the Religious Situation in the First State of Socialism: Number 3" (Shehuizhuyi chujijieduan zongjiao zhuang-kuang diaocha baogao xuanji: disanji) (Shanxi Research Group, Philosophy Department, Beijing University, completed in 1987, mimeograph), p. 75.

7. Ibid., pp. 75–76.

8. Ibid., 78.

9. Ibid., 99–103; the statement about equitable treatment of non-Catholics and Catholics is on p. 103.

10. Ibid., pp. 71–81.

11. Lattimore, *High Tartary,* p. 50.

12. My analysis of the ethnic dimensions of Chinese Catholicism is based partly on Donald L. Horowitz, *Ethnic Groups in Conflict* (Berkeley: University of California Press, 1985).

13. For the process by which Chinese Muslims became classified as an ethnic group, see Gladney, *Muslim Chinese,* pp. 65–115.

14. See Margery Wolf, *The House of Lim: A Study of a Chinese Farm Family* (New York: Appleton-Century-Crofts, 1968), pp. 23–44.

15. For an account of conflicts in the nineteenth century between local Catholic lay leadership and an authoritarian clergy, see Hanson, *Catholic Politics in China and Korea,* pp. 17–18. When missionaries returned to China after 1842, they often clashed with local lay leaders (*huizhang*), who, in the century since the missionaries had been expelled because of the Rites Controversy, exercised strong control, especially financial control, over local Catholic communities. The missionaries successfully struggled to reassert control. For an account of the roles of priests and paid catechists in the early twentieth century, see Wiest, *Maryknoll in China,* pp. 77–130. As Wiest notes, however, by the 1940s, the Maryknoll fathers and sisters, as well as other missionary groups, increasingly placed emphasis on a lay apostolate, including the Legion of Mary. "The Communist takeover did not permit much further development of the laity. Yet the groups in place proved to be strong" (p. 128). The history of the nineteenth century, however, suggests that if the Chinese Catholic Church were to reestablish a strong hierarchy, priests today might once again come into conflict with local leaders.

16. Wu Fei, "Zanmen shi fengjiaode: Huabei mouxiande tianzhujiao shequ" (We are Catholics: Catholic communities in a county of north China) (Department of Philosophy, Beijing University, 1996), pp. 13–16.

17. Ibid., p. 13.

18. For examples of the animosity that arises over the recovery of confiscated Church property and for the tendency of each side to demonize the other, see Ma Ji, "My Statement"; Underground Bishop, "My Vision of the Patriotic Association"; and Joseph Yao Tianmin, "Who Is Not Loyal to the Church?";

all in *The Catholic Church in Modern China,* ed. Edmond Tang and Jean-Paul Wiest (Maryknoll, N.Y.: Orbis Books, 1993), pp. 120–141. Father Yao is a Chinese priest from the Philippines who has visited Catholic communities in China and is sympathetic to the public Church. He accuses some outspoken underground Catholics of being "henchmen of Satan" (p. 138). Bishop Ma says that "believers" should "keep a distance" from members of the Chinese Catholic Patriotic Association "and fear their influence (as they would the devils and ghosts)" (p. 122). There is also a strong tendency for priests on both sides to accuse the others of breaking the vows of celibacy. In any case, for ordinary Catholics, one of the key signs of the legitimacy of a priest is whether he has remained celibate.

19. Some underground priests and bishops, however, do act clandestinely.

20. UCAN News, January 20, 1994.

21. This is, of course, a broad generalization. Context-specific factors can lead to sharp conflict even when, for example, a bishop is widely known to be approved by the Vatican. One such factor is rumor about the sexual behavior of bishops and priests in charge of particular communities. Some clergy on both the public and underground sides of the Church are rumored to have violated their vows of celibacy. Rumors about celibacy can open the way to serious struggles among factions.

Indeed, some priests have gotten married. In some cases they were pressured to do so during the Cultural Revolution; in other cases they decided to do so on their own. Such priests are widely rejected by the Catholic laity, even those priests who entered into marriages of convenience during the Cultural Revolution and never lived with their "spouse." Acknowledging the lack of legitimacy of married priests, the public Church has removed most of them from the pastoral ministry. It is widely rumored, however, that Bishop Fu Tieshan of Beijing, a prominent figure in the Chinese Catholic Patriotic Association, is married and has several children, which further undermines the legitimacy of the Chinese Catholic Patriotic Association in the eyes of most Catholics. See Richard Madsen, "The Catholic Church in China: Cultural Contradictions, Institutional Survival, and Religious Renewal," in *Unofficial China: Popular Culture and Thought in the People's Republic,* ed. Perry Link, Richard Madsen, and Paul G. Pickowicz (Boulder, Colo.: Westview Press, 1989), pp. 113–114.

22. Quoted in Wiest, *Maryknoll in China,* p. 120.

23. And sometimes, as noted in "Selected Reports," even Communist Party members become Catholic, in violation of Party regulations. The researchers describe one village in which two Party members pay "both Party dues and Mass stipends" (p. 87).

24. Ibid., pp. 71–98. The researchers note that in the village with a strong Catholic atmosphere, attendance at religious services is a family custom, "like watching TV in the evening is for many of us" (p. 79).

25. For recent Chinese histories of the Zhangzhuang cathedral and its associated community, see Zhang Pingyi and Kang Yu, "Xianxian zhangzhuang tianzhujiao congjiaotangde fandong huodong ye dai dongnan renminde fan di ai guo yundong," in *Hebei wenshi cikan xuanji,* vol. 1 ([Shijiazhuang:] Hebei

Renmin Chubanshe, 1980); and Pei Shulan, ed., *Tianzhutang zai Xianxian deng chude tianchan* (Tianjin: Jindaishi Cikan, Nankai University, 1992).

26. According to some estimates, over one hundred million rural people migrate to urban areas in search of at least temporary work. For further information on the floating population, see Dorothy J. Solinger, *China's Transients and the State: A Form of Civil Society?* (Shatin, HK: Hong Kong Institute of Asia-Pacific Studies, Chinese University of Hong Kong, 1991); and Dorothy J. Solinger, *China's Urban Transients and the Collapse of the Communist "Public Goods Regime": The Significance and Impact of Rural-to-Urban Migration during the Transition to Socialism* (Washington, D.C.: Woodrow Wilson International Center for Scholars, 1993).

27. With the help of the Holy Spirit Study Centre in Hong Kong, many of the best theologians from Hong Kong's Holy Spirit Seminary and from Taiwan's seminaries have gone to seminaries in the People's Republic to teach theology.

28. The Vatican is deliberately equivocal in its support of these various groups. In response to a circular letter distributed by the Cardinal Kung Foundation attacking the public Church and its foreign supporters, the Congregation for the Evangelization of Peoples has declared, "The Holy See has always maintained a great veneration for Cardinal Kung and remains deeply grateful to him for his heroic and exemplary fidelity in reference to the Roman Pontiff. On the other hand, the Foundation is a private institution, not involved in the responsibility of the Holy See. Its activities and statements on the situation of the Church in China are the sole responsibility of the Foundation." The letter goes on to state that the "Holy See duly appreciates what the Catholics of mainland China are doing in order to maintain and manifest their necessary union with the Successor of Peter, and cannot but encourage them to persevere in this attitude. On the other hand, the situation of those belonging to the 'Patriotic Association' is much more complex than what appears and is presented in the above-mentioned circular letter. It is for this reason that the Holy Father has not ceased to exhort the two groups to become reconciled to each other.

"For what concerns the economic assistance referred to in the same letter, the Congregation has been and remains always ready to assist the ecclesial needs of the faithful Catholics in mainland China."

Letter from the Apostolic Pro-Nuncio to the United States, His Excellency, the Most Reverend Agostino Cacciavillan, to Bishop Anthony Pilla, President of the National Conference of Catholic Bishops, March 5, 1996.

CHAPTER 3. MORALITY AND SPIRITUALITY

1. The term *spirituality* is taken from Catholic theology. For a summary of the usage of the term in Catholic discourse, see Walter Principe, "Toward Defining Spirituality," *Sciences Religieuses/Studies in Religion* 12, no. 2 (1983): 127–141. Basically, the term means the same as the anthropological term *ethos,* although Catholic theology has a more normative intent than anthropology—it wants to know what kind of ethos a Christian community should have rather than describe what it actually does have. I prefer to use the Catholic vernacular

term rather than the anthropological jargon in order to evoke a better feel for the communities that I am studying.

2. The Chinese language distinguishes different kinds of virtues that in English we would mostly lump together under "loyalty": for instance, *xiao,* or "filial piety," and *zhong,* or "loyalty to a sovereign." Confucian philosophy elaborates at great length the priorities and connections among these different virtues. Villagers do not make all these distinctions, however, and I have used the terms *family loyalty, community loyalty, loyalty to friends,* and so forth, to refer to virtues that are given distinctive words in the Chinese language.

3. See Robert N. Bellah, "Father and Son in Christianity and Confucianism," in *Beyond Belief: Essays on Religion in a Post-traditional World,* ed. Robert N. Bellah (New York: Harper & Row, 1970), pp. 77–99.

4. See Human Rights Watch/Asia, *Detained in China and Tibet: A Directory of Political and Religious Prisoners* (New York: Human Rights Watch, 1994).

5. Jean Charbonnier, "The 'Underground' Church," in *The Catholic Church in Modern China,* ed. Edmond Tang and Jean-Paul Wiest (Maryknoll, N.Y.: Orbis Books, 1993), p. 64. Father Charbonnier notes that "the faithful themselves see no great reason to object as the news they have received of events that occurred in June [1989] stresses the wisdom of government action on behalf of law and order."

6. The document is entitled "Thirteen Points" and is reprinted in Priest from Northern China, "The Present Chinese Church," in *The Catholic Church in Modern China,* ed. Edmond Tang and Jean-Paul Wiest (Maryknoll, N.Y.: Orbis Books, 1993), pp. 142–145. However, some priests sympathetic to the public Church have claimed that this document, attributed to Bishop Fan, was in fact written by extremists in the underground Church in the name of Bishop Fan and that Bishop Fan himself did not approve of all of it. It is impossible to verify this claim. Priest from Northern China, "The Present Chinese Church," p. 150.

7. "Selected Reports," p. 118.

8. *Acta Apostolicae Sedi,* vol. 2 (Rome: Typis Polyglottis Vaticanis, December 1, 1919), p. 446, as quoted in Wiest, *Maryknoll in China,* p. 74.

9. This view resonates with an authoritarian strand in Chinese political culture. Some Chinese intellectuals acknowledged and strongly criticized this cultural strand in the 1988 Chinese television documentary *Heshang* (Deathsong of the river) and were imprisoned or forced into exile after the crackdown of June 4, 1989. See Su Xiaokang and Wang Luxiang, *Deathsong of the River: A Reader's Guide to the Chinese TV Series Heshang,* trans. and ed. Richard W. Bodman and Pin P. Wang (Ithaca, N.Y.: Cornell East Asia Program, 1991).

10. "Selected Reports," p. 66. See also William Hinton, *Shen Fan* (New York: Vintage Books, 1984), pp. 278–282.

11. UCAN News, September 11, 1992.

12. Steven Mufson, "China's Catholics Defy Beijing's Ban: Illegal Masses Draw Throngs." *Washington Post,* 2 June 1995, p. A1.

13. David Blackbourne, *Marpingen: Apparitions of the Virgin Mary in 19th Century Germany* (New York: Knopf, 1994), p. 364.

14. Ibid., p. 374.

15. Generally, women pay much more attention to folk-religious rituals than men do. In the ethnographic study of Protestant communities in rural Guangdong carried out by May Ming-chun Cheng, women were far more active than men; May Ming-chun Cheng, "Christianity Fever: Contagion and Constraint of a Religious Movement in China," Ph.D. diss., Hong Kong University, 1996. But in the old Catholic villages in Shanxi described in the Beijing University study, men attended church almost as much as women; "Selected Reports."

16. Charbonnier, "The 'Underground' Church," p. 61.

CHAPTER 4. URBAN CATHOLICISM AND CIVIL SOCIETY

1. Yang Ni [pseud.], "Longqi: Dragon Prays," trans. by Norman Walling, S.J., *Tripod* 14, no. 82 (July–August 1994): 25.

2. Quoted in Richard Madsen, "Hierarchical Modernization: Tianjin's Gong Shang College as a Model for Catholic Community in North China," in *Becoming Chinese: Passages to Modernity and Beyond: 1900–1950*, ed. Yeh Wen-hsin (forthcoming). (The quotations are taken from materials in the French Jesuit archives.)

3. Madsen, "Hierarchical Modernization," p. 3. See also Ruth Hayhoe, "A Chinese Catholic Philosophy of Higher Education in Republican China," *Tripod* 48 (1988): 49–60.

4. This quote and the other information in this paragraph were gathered at a conference, "The Yanjing Experience and Higher Education in China," organized by Arthur Rosenbaum at Claremont McKenna College, May 1996.

5. Madsen, "Hierarchical Modernization."

6. For an excellent account of Catholic political power in Shanghai, see Hanson, *Catholic Politics in China and Korea*, pp. 72–84.

7. Andrew G. Walder, *Communist Neo-traditionalism: Work and Authority in Chinese Industry* (Berkeley: University of California Press, 1986).

8. Andrew G. Walder, "Organized Dependency and Cultures of Authority in Chinese Industry," *Journal of Asian Studies* 43, no. 1 (November 1983): 68.

9. Anthony Lam, "The Spirit of Vatican II in the Church in China," *Tripod* 74 (1993): 23–33.

10. Bishop Aloysius Jin Luxian, "How the 'Little Flock' in China Lives the Gospel in the Changing Society of Today," speech at a conference in Manila, 1994; Xeroxed English text furnished by the Holy Spirit Study Centre in Hong Kong, p. 4.

11. According to "China Church Update," *Tripod* 13, no. 77 (September–October 1993), "On August 4, 1993, Buddhists, Catholics, Protestants, and Taoists in Shanghai formed the Shanghai Zhongxin Real Estate Development Company. . . . The local Catholic church, says the chancellor, owns about one-third of the 1.3 million square meters of land and property that the new company hopes to develop. The enterprise has already attracted property developers from Hong Kong and signed contracts with at least two firms to rebuild a church and to construct commercial buildings. Bishop Aloysius Jin Luxian, the chairman of the company's board of directors, says that the profit from the real estate development will enable the diocese to be self-supporting and also pro-

vide services to the poor. Some people have expressed dismay that the churches would be so willing, as the Chinese saying goes, 'to jump into the sea.' They wonder if it is ever good for the church to move beyond religion to business interests" (p. 65).

12. I have discussed these issues in detail in Richard Madsen, "God, Money, and Modernity: Catholic Response to the Consumer Ethic," unpublished paper, 1997. See *The Consumer Revolution in Urban China,* ed. Deborah S. Davis (Berkeley: University of California Press, forthcoming) for further analyses of China's emerging consumer culture.

13. Jin Luxian, "How the 'Little Flock' in China," pp. 3–4.

14. Jonathan D. Spence, *The Memory Palace of Matteo Ricci* (New York: Viking Penguin, 1984).

15. Yang Ni, "Longqi." The Chinese text of this story—which was originally published in the Hong Kong publication *Zhu Ai Zhong Hua* in five segments from May through September 1993—is also provided in the July–August 1994 edition of *Tripod;* I have made slight modifications in the English translation based on my reading of the Chinese.

16. Ibid., pp. 5–27. This story has provoked some lively reactions from Chinese Catholics in Hong Kong and on the mainland. See Pandora Khor, "The Dragon Prays—A Reflection," *Tripod* 14, no. 82 (July–August 1994): 28–30; and Le Sheng, "After Reading Longqi: Dragon Prays—A Reflection on the Church in China," in *The Role of the Church in China's Modernization Drive* (Hong Kong: Hong Kong Catholic Truth Society, 1995), pp. 251–280.

17. Maria Goretti Lau, "The Formation of New Church Leaders," in *The Catholic Church in Modern China,* ed. Edmond Tang and Jean-Paul Wiest (Maryknoll, N.Y.: Orbis Books, 1993), p. 74; and Priest from Northern China, "The Present Chinese Church." Speaking of underground priests in Xian County, this priest writes, "With a few exceptions, most of these priests are poorly educated. . . . These underground seminarians not only lack cultural knowledge, they also lack knowledge of the church. They studied for a few months under [underground Bishop] Li [Zhenrong] and were ordained priests. When they studied canon law, they chose the chapter on excommunication and specialized in excommunication in order to preach about the excommunication of bishops and priests. They memorized all these points but neglected to study the requirements and qualifications for priesthood" (p. 148).

18. Jin Luxian, "How the 'Little Flock' in China," p. 3.

19. Ibid., pp. 5–6.

20. For a condemnation of Bishop Jin, see Underground Bishop, "My Vision of the Patriotic Association," p. 131. Bishop Jin has not joined the Chinese Catholic Patriotic Association, but he is willing to work within the government's regulations about religion. The anonymous underground bishop says that such men "are more dangerous than those who join the [Chinese Catholic Patriotic Association] openly. They are more deceitful. In their inner hearts, they are patriots who have separated from the pope!"

21. The address was given on January 14, 1995, on the silver jubilee of Radio Veritas Asia in Manila. UCAN News.

CHAPTER 5. THE CATHOLIC
CHURCH AND CIVIL SOCIETY

1. Taylor, "Modes of Civil Society." See also Victor M. Perez-Diaz, *The Return of Civil Society: The Emergence of Democratic Spain* (Cambridge, Mass.: Harvard University Press, 1993), pp. 54–107.

2. The Vatican did negotiate such agreements with Eastern European governments in the 1970s as a part of its "Ostpolitik." The Vatican also followed this policy in Vietnam. See Eric O. Hanson, *The Catholic Church in World Politics* (Princeton, N.J.: Princeton University Press, 1987), pp. 197–233; and Hanson, *Catholic Politics in China and Korea*, pp. 114–116. As Hanson points out, however, an obstacle to the Vatican's making such an arrangement with the People's Republic of China is that the Church in China is much smaller than the Church in Vietnam and many Eastern European countries; as a result the Vatican has less leverage with the Chinese government than it had with East European socialist governments and with the Vietnamese government.

3. Currently, the most vocal example of such a group in U.S. politics is the Family Research Council, whose constituency is based in the Christian right. Together with other "neoconservative" groups, the Council has lobbied successfully for the creation of the State Department's Advisory Committee on Religious Freedom Abroad (which is balanced with representatives of non-Christian faiths and includes members not sympathetic to the Christian right's agenda). In 1997, the Christian neoconservatives lobbied against the renewal of Most Favored Nation trading status with China because of China's persecution of Catholic and Protestant Christians. They have also promoted the Freedom from Religious Persecution Act, which would create an office to monitor religious persecution and sanction countries engaged in persecution. In keeping with the strand of ascetic Protestantism from which such groups are descended, they are strongly suspicious of any form of state regulation, even within the United States. See Bellah et al., *Habits of the Heart,* p. x.

4. The chair of the House of Representatives International Human Rights Subcommittee, Congressman Chris Smith (Republican, New Jersey), for instance, visited China in 1994 accompanied by Joseph Kung, nephew of Cardinal Gong Pinmei and president of the Cardinal Kung Foundation. In the course of his visit, he had a meeting with underground Bishop Cosmos Shu Zhiming, who was arrested almost immediately after the visit. Citing this incident, as well as many other human-rights abuses against religious leaders, Congressman Smith has been one of the most vigorous advocates for cutting off most forms of exchanges with China, including economic ones. (See the account of this trip by Patricia Zapor, Catholic News Service, 1994.) Critics of Congressman Smith might argue that by meeting with Bishop Shu he provided a good excuse for the Chinese authorities to put the bishop in prison and that the economic and political sanctions proposed against China by Congressman Smith may not improve the practice of Catholicism in China and, by complicating the integration of China into the world community, may postpone the advent of effective religious freedom there.

5. See Hsin-huang Michael Hsiao, "The Development and Organization of Foundations in Taiwan: An Expression of Cultural Vigor in a Newly Born Society," in *Quiet Revolutions on Taiwan, Republic of China*, ed. Jason C. Hu (Taipei: Kwang Hwa, 1994), pp. 386–419; and Makito Noda, "Philanthropy and NGOs in Hong Kong and Asia Pacific Orientation," in *Emerging Civil Society in the Asia Pacific Community: Nongovernmental Underpinnings of the Emerging Asia Pacific Regional Community*, ed. Tadashi Yamamoto (Singapore and Tokyo: Institute of Southeast Asian Studies and Japan Centre for International Exchange, 1995), pp. 111–120.

6. Gellner, *Conditions of Liberty*, p. 60; emphasis in the original.

7. Ibid., p. 86.

8. Lydia H. Liu, *Translingual Practice: Literature, National Culture, and Translated Modernity—China, 1900–1937* (Stanford, Calif.: Stanford University Press, 1995), p. 336.

9. A local peasant movement inspired by a local, charismatic would-be emperor is analyzed in Ann S. Anagnost, "The Beginning and End of an Emperor: A Counterrepresentation of the State," *Modern China* 11, no. 2 (April 1985): 147–176. The newsletter *China Focus*, published by the exiled journalist Liu Binyan under the auspices of the Princeton China Initiative, has published a stream of articles about rural unrest. See, for example, 3, no. 12 (December 1995); 4, no. 9 (September 1996); 4, no. 12 (December 1996); 5, no. 5 (May 1997).

10. Dali L. Yang, "The State and 'Uncivil Society': China's Growing Drug Problem in Comparative Perspective," paper presented at the meetings of the Association for Asian Studies, Boston, March 1993.

11. Shi Yuankang, "Shimin shehui yu zhongben yimo—Zhongguo xiandai daolushang de zhangai" (Civil society and the policy of "emphasizing the fundamental and repressing the secondary"—an obstacle in China's road to modernization), *Ershiyi Shiji* 6 (August 1991): 105–120; Wang Shaoguang, "Guanyu 'shimin shehui' de jidian sikao" (Reflections on the notion of "civil society"), *Ershiyi Shiji* 6 (December 1991): 102–114; and William T. Rowe, "The Problem of 'Civil Society' in Late Imperial China," *Modern China* 19, no. 2 (April 1993): 142.

12. Mayfair Yang, *Gifts, Favors, and Banquets: The Art of Social Relationships in China* (Ithaca, N.Y.: Cornell University Press, 1994). Yang argues that the "art of interpersonal relations (*guanxi*) represents a means of creating a self-governing *minjian* society that could become a Chinese equivalent of a civil society" (p. 288). I think that this may be possible in a modernized, urban Chinese context but not in the rural hinterlands, where *guanxi* is too often connected with corrupt, unaccountable control by the powerful over the weak or with forms of belligerent "localism" (or with both).

13. Alexis de Tocqueville, *Democracy in America*, ed. J. P. Mayer, trans. George Lawrence (Garden City, N.Y.: Doubleday Anchor, 1969), p. 508.

14. As Mead has put it, "One of the most widely accepted maxims of political science states that a liberal democracy of the Western type requires, above all, a strong middle class." Walter Russell Mead, *Mortal Splendor: The American Empire in Transition* (Boston: Houghton Mifflin, 1987), p. 23. An earlier

argument to the same effect was proposed by Seymour Martin Lipset, *Political Man: The Social Bases of Politics* (Garden City, N.Y.: Anchor Books, 1963).

15. Zhang Ye, "Chinese NGOs: A Survey Report," in *Emerging Civil Society in the Asia Pacific Community: Nongovernmental Underpinnings of the Emerging Asia Pacific Regional Community,* ed. Tadashi Yamamoto (Singapore and Tokyo: Institute of Southeast Asian Studies and Japan Centre for International Exchange, 1995), pp. 93–107.

16. See, for example, David Wank, "Bureaucratic Patronage and Private Business: Changing Networks of Power in Urban China," in *The Waning of the Communist State: Economic Origins of Political Decline in China and Hungary,* ed. Andrew G. Walder (Berkeley: University of California Press, 1995), pp. 153–183.

17. See John King Fairbank, *The Great Chinese Revolution, 1800–1985* (New York: Harper & Row, 1986), pp. 167–239.

18. Fareed Zakaria, "At Hour of Triumph, Democracy Recedes as the Global Ideal," *New York Times,* 18 February 1996, sect. 4, pp. 1, 5.

19. Sullivan, "The Infrastructure of Democracy."

20. Putnam, *Making Democracy Work,* pp. 87–90.

21. Ibid., p. 107.

22. Emile Durkheim, *The Elementary Forms of the Religious Life* (New York: Free Press, 1968).

23. Bi Ming, "'Christianity Fever': in China," *Tripod* 14, no. 83 (September–October 1994): 6–14; and Bi Ming, "'Christianity Fever' Journalists Investigate and Report," *Tripod* 14, no. 83 (September–October 1994): 15–30. "Christianity" in Chinese (*jidu jiao*) means Protestantism as opposed to Catholicism (*tianzhu jiao*). Also, see Cheng, "Christianity Fever."

24. More books have been written about the Protestant Church in China than about the Catholic Church. Notable among them are Hunter and Chan, *Protestantism in Contemporary China;* Tony Lambert, *The Resurrection of the Chinese Church* (London: Hodder and Stoughton, 1991); and Philip L. Wickeri, *Seeking the Common Ground: Protestant Christianity, the Three-Self Movement, and China's United Front* (Maryknoll, NY: Orbis Books, 1988).

25. Max Weber, *The Sociology of Religion,* trans. Ephraim Fischoff (Boston: Beacon Press, 1964).

26. Second Vatican Council, *Lumen Gentium* (Dogmatic constitution on the Church), November 21, 1964; *Dei Verbum* (Dogmatic constitution on divine revelation), November 18, 1965; *Dignitatis Humanae* (Declaration on religious freedom), December 7, 1965; *Gaudium et Spes* (Pastoral constitution on the Church in the modern world), December 7, 1965; all published by the United States Catholic Conference Office of Publishing and Promotion Services, Washington, D.C.

27. John Paul II, *The Gospel of Life (Evangelium Vitae)* (New York: Random House, Times Books, 1995), pp. 127–128.

28. The Vatican, at least, is continuing to reach out to the Chinese government. In a speech broadcast to Asia on December 3, 1996, the pope made a new appeal to the Chinese government to normalize relations with the Vatican. He stated that there should be no conflict between faith and "any political or-

der" and said China should not "be afraid either of God or his Church." "I therefore ask [China], with a sense of deference, to respect the authentic freedom which is the birthright of every man and woman and to allow believers in Christ to be able to contribute their energies and talents to the development of the nation," the pope said. "The Chinese nation has an important role to play in the bosom of the community of nations. Catholics can lend significant support to that and they will do so with enthusiasm and dedication" (Reuters).

29. Statistics from Charbonnier, *Guide to the Catholic Church in China.*

30. Information based on interviews conducted with priests on Taiwan in 1994 and 1996.

31. Hsiao, "The Development and Organization of Foundations in Taiwan."

32. A brief description is in Hsin-huang Michael Hsiao, "The Emerging Asia Pacific Regional Activities of Taiwan's Foundations," in *Emerging Civil Society in the Asia Pacific Community: Nongovernmental Underpinnings of the Emerging Asia Pacific Regional Community,* ed. Tadashi Yamamoto (Singapore and Tokyo: Institute of Southeast Asian Studies and Japan Centre for International Exchange, 1995), pp. 625–635.

33. Julio de Santa Ana, "Areas of Convergence and Areas of Questioning," in *Documentation of the Consultation on Theology and Civil Society,* ed. Fritz Erich Anhelm (Locuum, Germany: Evangelische Akademie Locuum, 1996), pp. 182–183.

Bibliography

"An Accurate and Truthful Survey Report: Assessment of 'Present Situation of and Reflections on the Catholic Church in Villages around Tianjin.'" *China Study Journal* 6, no. 3 (1991): 45–48.

Amnesty International. *Urgent Action.* New York: Amnesty International, 1995.

Anagnost, Ann S. "The Beginning and End of an Emperor: A Counterrepresentation of the State." *Modern China* 11, no. 2 (April 1985): 147–176.

Asia Watch. *Continuing Religious Repression in China.* New York: Asia Watch, 1993.

Bellah, Robert N. "Father and Son in Christianity and Confucianism." In *Beyond Belief: Essays on Religion in a Post-traditional World,* by Robert N. Bellah. New York: Harper & Row, 1970.

Bellah, Robert N., Richard Madsen, William M. Sullivan, Ann Swidler, and Steven M. Tipton. *Habits of the Heart: Individualism and Commitment in American Life.* Rev. ed. Berkeley: University of California Press, 1996.

Bi Ming, "'Christianity Fever': in China." *Tripod* 14, no. 83 (September–October 1994): 6–14.

———. "'Christianity Fever' Journalists Investigate and Report." *Tripod* 14, no. 83 (September–October 1994): 15–30.

Blackbourne, David. *Marpingen: Apparitions of the Virgin Mary in 19th Century Germany.* New York: Knopf, 1994.

Bush, Richard C., Jr. *Religion in Communist China.* Nashville, Tenn.: Abingdon Press, 1970.

Cary-Elwes, Columba. *China and the Cross: A Survey of Missionary History.* New York: P. J. Kennedy and Sons, 1957.

Chan, Kim-kwong. *Struggling for Survival: The Catholic Church in China from 1949–1970.* Hong Kong: Christian Study Centre on Religion and Culture, 1992.

————. *Towards a Contextual Ecclesiology: The Catholic Church in the People's Republic of China (1979–1983): Its Life and Theological Implications.* Hong Kong: Photech Systems, 1987.

Charbonnier, Jean. *Guide to the Catholic Church in China.* Singapore: China Catholic Communication, 1997.

————. "The 'Underground' Church." In *The Catholic Church in Modern China,* edited by Edmond Tang and Jean-Paul Wiest. Maryknoll, N.Y.: Orbis Books, 1993.

Cheng, May Ming-chun. "Christianity Fever: Contagion and Constraint of a Religious Movement in China." Ph.D. diss., Hong Kong University, 1996.

Ci, Jiwei. *Dialectic of the Chinese Revolution: From Utopianism to Hedonism.* Stanford, Calif.: Stanford University Press, 1994.

Cohen, Jean, and Andrew Arato. *Civil Society and Political Theory.* Cambridge, Mass.: MIT Press, 1992.

Cohen, Paul A. *China and Christianity: The Missionary Movement and the Growth of Chinese Antiforeignism, 1860–1870.* Ann Arbor: University of Michigan Press, 1963.

Cummins, J. S. *A Question of Rites: Friar Domingo Navarrete and the Jesuits in China.* Aldershot, Hants.: Scolar, 1993.

De Gendt, Rik. *A New Life for the Church in China.* Manila: Bookmark, 1990.

Ding, X. L. *The Decline of Communism in China: Legitimacy Crisis, 1977–1989.* Cambridge: Cambridge University Press, 1994.

————. "Institutional Amphibiousness and the Transition from Communism: The Case of China." *British Journal of Political Science* 24, pt. 3 (July 1994): 293–317.

Dumont, Louis. *Homo Hierarchicus: An Essay on the Caste System.* Translated by Mark Sainsbury. Chicago: University of Chicago Press, 1970.

Dunne, George H., S.J. *Generation of Giants: The Story of the Jesuits in China in the Last Decades of the Ming Dynasty.* Notre Dame, Ind.: University of Notre Dame Press, 1962.

Durkheim, Emile. *The Elementary Forms of the Religious Life.* New York: Free Press, 1968.

Esherick, Joseph W. *The Origins of the Boxer Uprising.* Berkeley: University of California Press, 1987.

Fairbank, John King. *The Great Chinese Revolution, 1800–1985.* New York: Harper & Row, 1986.

Family News of the Catholic Church in China. Hong Kong: Holy Spirit Study Centre, 1990.

Freeman, L. C., and D. Ruan. "An International Comparative Study of Interpersonal Behavior and Role Relationships." *L'Année Sociologique* 47: 89–115.

Galston, William A. "Won't You Be My Neighbor?" *American Prospect* 26 (May–June 1996): 16–18.

Gellner, Ernest. *Conditions of Liberty: Civil Society and Its Rivals*. New York: Penguin Books, 1994.

Gladney, Dru C. *Muslim Chinese: Ethnic Nationalism in the People's Republic*. Cambridge, Mass.: Harvard University Council on East Asian Studies, 1991.

Hanson, Eric O. *The Catholic Church in World Politics*. Princeton, N.J.: Princeton University Press, 1987.

———. *Catholic Politics in China and Korea*. Maryknoll, N.Y.: Orbis Books, 1980.

Harrison, Ray. *Bishop Walsh of Maryknoll: Prisoner of Red China*. New York: Putnam, 1962.

Havel, Vaclav. "Remarks upon Receiving the Philadelphia Liberty Medal in Independence Hall, July 4, 1994." In *The Art of the Impossible: Politics as Morality and Practice: Speeches and Writings, 1990–1996*. New York: Knopf, 1997.

Hayhoe, Ruth. "A Chinese Catholic Philosophy of Higher Education in Republican China." *Tripod* 48 (1988): 49–60.

Hinton, William. *Shen Fan*. New York: Vintage Books, 1984.

Horowitz, Donald L. *Ethnic Groups in Conflict*. Berkeley: University of California Press, 1985.

Hsiao, Hsin-huang Michael. "The Development and Organization of Foundations in Taiwan: An Expression of Cultural Vigor in a Newly Born Society." In *Quiet Revolutions on Taiwan, Republic of China*, edited by Jason C. Hu. Taipei: Kwang Hwa, 1994.

———. "The Emerging Asia Pacific Regional Activities of Taiwan's Foundations." In *Emerging Civil Society in the Asia Pacific Community: Nongovernmental Underpinnings of the Emerging Asia Pacific Regional Community*, edited by Tadashi Yamamoto. Singapore and Tokyo: Institute of Southeast Asian Studies and Japan Centre for International Exchange, 1995.

Human Rights Watch/Asia. *Detained in China and Tibet: A Directory of Political and Religious Prisoners*. New York: Human Rights Watch, 1994.

Hunter, Alan, and Kim-kwong Chan. *Protestantism in Contemporary China*. Cambridge: Cambridge University Press, 1993.

John Paul II. *The Gospel of Life (Evangelium Vitae)*. New York: Random House/Times Books, 1995.

Keane, John. *Democracy and Civil Society*. New York: Verso, 1988.

Khor, Pandora. "The Dragon Prays—A Reflection." *Tripod* 14, no. 82 (1994): 28–30.

Ladany, Laszlo. *The Catholic Church in China*. New York: Freedom House, 1987.

Lam, Anthony. "How Many Catholics Are There in China?" *Tripod* 71 (September–October 1992): 51–57.

———. "The Spirit of Vatican II in the Church in China." *Tripod* 74 (1993): 23–33.

Lambert, Tony. *The Resurrection of the Chinese Church*. London: Hodder and Stoughton, 1991.

Latourette, Kenneth Scott. *A History of Christian Missions in China.* New York: Macmillan, 1929.

Lattimore, Owen. *High Tartary.* 1930. Reprint, New York: Kodansha International, 1994.

Lau, Maria Goretti. "The Formation of New Church Leaders." In *The Catholic Church in Modern China,* edited by Edmond Tang and Jean-Paul Wiest. Maryknoll, N.Y.: Orbis Books, 1993.

Le Sheng. "After Reading Longqi: Dragon Prays—A Reflection on the Church in China." In *The Role of the Church in China's Modernization Drive.* Hong Kong: Hong Kong Catholic Truth Society, 1995.

Leung, Beatrice. *Sino-Vatican Relations: Problems in Conflicting Authority, 1976–1986.* Cambridge: Cambridge University Press, 1992.

Lipset, Seymour Martin. *Political Man: The Social Bases of Politics.* Garden City, N.Y.: Anchor Books, 1963.

Litzinger, Charles A. "Rural Religion and Village Organization in North China: The Catholic Challenge in the Late Nineteenth Century." In *Christianity in China: From the Eighteenth Century to the Present,* edited by Daniel H. Bays. Stanford, Calif.: Stanford University Press, 1996.

Liu, Lydia H. *Translingual Practice: Literature, National Culture, and Translated Modernity—China, 1900–1937.* Stanford, Calif.: Stanford University Press, 1995.

Living Temples. Video produced by the Kuangch'i Program Service, Taipei, 1991.

Luhrmann, T. M. "The Ugly Goddess: Reflections on the Role of Violent Images in Religious Experience." Unpublished paper, University of California, San Diego, 1996.

Luo Zhufeng, ed. *Religion under Socialist China* (Zhongguo shehui zhuyi shiqide zhongjiao wenti). English translation by Donald E. MacInnis and Zheng Xi'an. Armonk, N.Y.: Sharpe, 1991.

Ma Ji. "My Statement." In *The Catholic Church in Modern China,* edited by Edmond Tang and Jean-Paul Wiest. Maryknoll, N.Y.: Orbis Books, 1993.

MacInnis, Donald E. *Religion in China Today: Policy and Practice.* Maryknoll, N.Y.: Orbis Books, 1989.

———. *Religious Policy and Practice in Communist China.* New York: Macmillan, 1972.

Madsen, Richard. "The Catholic Church in China: Cultural Contradictions, Institutional Survival, and Religious Renewal." In *Unofficial China: Popular Culture and Thought in the People's Republic,* edited by Perry Link, Richard Madsen, and Paul G. Pickowicz. Boulder, Colo.: Westview Press, 1989.

———. "The Catholic Church in China Today: A New Rites Controversy?" In *The Chinese Rites Controversy: Its History and Meaning,* edited by D. E. Mungello. Sankt Augustin, Germany: Institut Monumenta Serica, 1994.

———. "Community, Civil Society, and Social Ecology." In *Report from Euro-American Workshop.* Forthcoming.

———. "God, Money, and Modernity: Catholic Response to the Consumer Ethic." Unpublished paper, University of California, San Diego, 1997.

———. "Hierarchical Modernization: Tianjin's Gong Shang College as a Model

for Catholic Community in North China." In *Becoming Chinese: Passages to Modernity and Beyond: 1900–1950,* edited by Yeh Wen-hsin. Forthcoming.
———. *Morality and Power in a Chinese Village.* Berkeley: University of California Press, 1994.

Mead, Walter Russell. *Mortal Splendor: The American Empire in Transition.* Boston: Houghton Mifflin, 1987.

Minamiki, George, S.J. *The Chinese Rites Controversy: From Its Beginnings to Modern Times.* Chicago: Loyola University Press, 1985.

Mungello, D. E., ed. *The Chinese Rites Controversy: Its History and Meaning.* Sankt Augustin, Germany: Monumenta Serica, 1994.

Noda, Makito. "Philanthropy and NGOs in Hong Kong and Asia Pacific Orientation." In *Emerging Civil Society in the Asia Pacific Community: Nongovernmental Underpinnings of the Emerging Asia Pacific Regional Community,* edited by Tadashi Yamamoto. Singapore and Tokyo: Institute of Southeast Asian Studies and Japan Centre for International Exchange, 1995.

The Official Handbook of the Legion of Mary. Louisville, Ky.: Publishers Printing, 1953.

Overmeyer, Daniel L. *Religions of China.* New York: Harper & Row, 1986.

Palmer, G. *God's Underground in Asia.* New York: Appleton-Century-Crofts, 1953.

Pei Shulan, ed. *Tianzhutang zai xianxian deng chude tianchan.* Tianjin: Jindaishi Cikan, Nankai University, 1992.

Perez-Diaz, Victor M. *The Return of Civil Society: The Emergence of Democratic Spain.* Cambridge, Mass.: Harvard University Press, 1993.

Portes, Alejandro, and Patricia Landolt. "The Downside of Social Capital." *American Prospect* 26 (May–June 1996): 16–21.

Priest from Northern China. "The Present Chinese Church." In *The Catholic Church in Modern China,* edited by Edmond Tang and Jean-Paul Wiest. Maryknoll, N.Y.: Orbis Books, 1993.

Principe, Walter. "Toward Defining Spirituality." *Sciences Religieuses/Studies in Religion* 12, no. 2 (1983): 127–141.

Putnam, Robert D. "Bowling Alone: America's Declining Social Capital." *Journal of Democracy* 6, no. 1 (January 1995): 65–78.

———. *Making Democracy Work: Civic Traditions in Modern Italy.* Princeton, N.J.: Princeton University Press, 1993.

———. "The Strange Disappearance of Civic America." *American Prospect* 24 (Winter 1996): 34–48.

Ross, Andrew C. *A Vision Betrayed: The Jesuits in Japan and China, 1542–1742.* Maryknoll, N.Y.: Orbis Books, 1994.

Rowe, William T. "The Problem of 'Civil Society' in Late Imperial China." *Modern China* 19, no. 2 (April 1993): 139–157.

Ruan, D., X. Dai, W. Zhang, Y. Pan, and L. C. Freeman. "Suppose You Gave a Survey and Everybody Came." *Cultural Anthropology Methods* 6: 12.

Ruan, D., L. C. Freeman, X. Dai, Y. Pan, and W. Zhang. "On the Changing Structure of Social Networks in Urban China." *Social Networks* 19: 75–89.

Santa Ana, Julio de. "Areas of Convergence and Areas of Questioning." In *Documentation of the Consultation on Theology and Civil Society,* edited by

Fritz Erich Anhelm. Locuum, Germany: Evangelische Akademie Locuum, 1996.

Schudson, Michael. "What If Civic Life Didn't Die?" *American Prospect* 25 (March–April 1996): 17–25.

Second Vatican Council. *Dei Verbum* (Dogmatic constitution on divine revelation). Washington, D.C.: United States Catholic Conference Office of Publishing and Promotion Services, 1965.

———. *Dignitatis Humanae* (Declaration on religious freedom). Washington, D.C.: United States Catholic Conference Office of Publishing and Promotion Services, 1965.

———. *Gaudium et Spes* (Pastoral constitution on the Church in the modern world). Washington, D.C: United States Catholic Conference Office of Publishing and Promotion Services, 1965.

———. *Lumen Gentium* (Dogmatic constitution on the Church). Washington, D.C.: United States Catholic Conference Office of Publishing and Promotion Services, 1964.

"Selected Reports on Investigations of the Religious Situation in the First Stage of Socialism: Number 3" (Shehuizhuyi chujijieduan zongjiao zhuangkuang diaocha baogao xuanji: disanji). Shanxi Research Group, Philosophy Department, Beijing University, completed in 1987. Mimeographed.

Shi Guoming et al. "Sunan diqu yumin xinyang tianzhujiao wenti chutan" (Preliminary study of Catholic fishermen in the Sunan area). *Zongjiao* 6 (November 1984): 36–42.

Shi Yuankang. "Shimin shehui yu zhongben yimo—Zhongguo xiandai daolushang de zhangai" (Civil society and the policy of "emphasizing the fundamental and repressing the secondary"—an obstacle in China's road to modernization). *Ershiyi Shiji* 6 (August 1991): 105–120.

Skocpol, Theda. "Unravelling from Above." *American Prospect* 25 (March–April 1996): 20–25.

Solinger, Dorothy J. *China's Transients and the State: A Form of Civil Society?* Shatin: HK Hong Kong Institute of Asia-Pacific Studies, Chinese University of Hong Kong, 1991.

———. *China's Urban Transients and the Collapse of the Communist "Public Goods Regime": The Significance and Impact of Rural-to-Urban Migration during the Transition to Socialism.* Washington, D.C.: Woodrow Wilson International Center for Scholars, 1993.

Spence, Jonathan D. *The Memory Palace of Matteo Ricci.* New York: Viking Penguin, 1984.

Spring Rain. Hong Kong: Holy Spirit Study Centre, 1990.

St. Sure, Donald F., S.J., trans. *100 Roman Documents concerning the Chinese Rites Controversy (1645–1941).* San Francisco: Ricci Institute, University of San Francisco, 1992.

Su Xiaokang. "My Views on a 'Sense of Mission.'" *Qiu Shi* 2 (1988): 47–48. Translated in Su Xiaokang and Wang Luxiang, *Deathsong of the River: A Reader's Guide to the Chinese TV Series Heshang.* Translated and edited by Richard W. Bodman and Pin P. Wan. Ithaca, N.Y.: Cornell University East Asia Program, 1991.

Su Xiaokang and Wang Luxiang. *Deathsong of the River: A Reader's Guide to the Chinese TV Series Heshang.* Translated and edited by Richard W. Bodman and Pin P. Wang. Ithaca, N.Y.: Cornell University East Asia Program, 1991.

Sullivan, William M. "The Infrastructure of Democracy: From Civil Society to Civic Community." Unpublished paper, La Salle University, n.d.

Tang, Edmond. "The Church into the 1990s." In *The Catholic Church in Modern China,* edited by Edmond Tang and Jean-Paul Wiest. Maryknoll, N.Y.: Orbis Books, 1993.

Tang, Edmond, and Jean-Paul Wiest, eds. *The Catholic Church in Modern China.* Maryknoll, N.Y.: Orbis Books, 1993.

Taylor, Charles. "Modes of Civil Society." *Public Culture* 3, no. 1 (Fall 1990): 95–131.

Thompson, Roger R. "Twilight of the Gods in the Chinese Countryside: Christians, Confucians, and the Modernizing State, 1861–1911." In *Christianity in China: From the Eighteenth Century to the Present,* edited by Daniel H. Bays. Stanford, Calif.: Stanford University Press, 1996.

Tocqueville, Alexis de. *Democracy in America.* Edited by J. P. Mayer. Translated by George Lawrence. Garden City, N.Y.: Doubleday Anchor, 1969.

Tong, John. "The Church from 1949 to 1990." In *The Catholic Church in Modern China,* edited by Edmond Tang and Jean-Paul Wiest. Maryknoll, N.Y.: Orbis Books, 1993.

Townsend, James. *Political Participation in Communist China.* Berkeley: University of California Press, 1967.

Underground Bishop. "My Vision of the Patriotic Association." In *The Catholic Church in Modern China,* edited by Edmond Tang and Jean-Paul Wiest. Maryknoll, N.Y.: Orbis Books, 1993.

Vallely, Richard M. "Couch-Potato Democracy?" *American Prospect* 25 (March–April 1996): 25–26.

Walder, Andrew G. *Communist Neo-traditionalism: Work and Authority in Chinese Industry.* Berkeley: University of California Press, 1986.

———. "Organized Dependency and Cultures of Authority in Chinese Industry." *Journal of Asian Studies* 43, no. 1 (November 1983): 51–76.

Walzer, Michael. "The Idea of Civil Society." *Dissent* 38, no. 2 (Spring 1991): 293–304.

Wang Shaoguang, "Guanyu 'shimin shehui' de jidian sikao" (Reflections on the notion of "civil society"). *Ershiyi Shiji* 6 (December 1991): 102–114.

Wank, David. "Bureaucratic Patronage and Private Business: Changing Networks of Power in Urban China." In *The Waning of the Communist State: Economic Origins of Political Decline in China and Hungary,* edited by Andrew G. Walder. Berkeley: University of California Press, 1995.

Weber, Max. *The Sociology of Religion.* Translated by Ephraim Fischoff. Boston: Beacon Press, 1964.

Wickeri, Philip L. *Seeking the Common Ground: Protestant Christianity, the Three-Self Movement, and China's United Front.* Maryknoll, N.Y.: Orbis Books, 1988.

Wiest, Jean-Paul. *Maryknoll in China.* Armonk, N.Y.: Sharpe, 1988.

Wolf, Margery. *The House of Lim: A Study of a Chinese Farm Family*. New York: Appleton-Century-Crofts, 1968.

Wu Fei. "Zanmen shi fengjiaode: Huabei mouxiande tianzhujiao shequ" (We are Catholics: Catholic communities in a county of north China). Department of Philosophy, Beijing University, 1996.

Yamamoto, Tadashi, ed. *Emerging Civil Society in the Asia Pacific Community: Nongovernmental Underpinnings of the Emerging Asia Pacific Regional Community*. Singapore and Tokyo: Institute of Southeast Asian Studies and Japan Centre for International Exchange, 1995.

Yang, C. K. *Religion in Chinese Society*. Berkeley: University of California Press, 1961.

Yang, Dali L. "The State and 'Uncivil Society': China's Growing Drug Problem in Comparative Perspective." Paper presented at the meetings of the Association for Asian Studies, Boston, March 1993.

Yang, Mayfair. *Gifts, Favors, and Banquets: The Art of Social Relationships in China*. Ithaca, N.Y.: Cornell University Press, 1994.

Yang Ni [pseud.]. "Longqi: Dragon Prays." Translated by Norman Walling, S.J. *Tripod* 14, no. 82 (July–August 1994): 5–27.

Yanjie Bian and John R. Logan. "Market Transition and the Persistence of Power: The Changing Stratification System in Urban China." *American Sociological Review* 61, no. 5 (October 1996): 739–758.

Yao Tianmin, Joseph. "Who Is Not Loyal to the Church?" In *The Catholic Church in Modern China*, edited by Edmond Tang and Jean-Paul Wiest. Maryknoll, N.Y.: Orbis Books, 1993.

Young, Ernest P. "The Politics of Evangelism at the End of the Qing: Nanchang, 1906." In *Christianity in China: From the Eighteenth Century to the Present*, edited by Daniel H. Bays. Stanford, Calif.: Stanford University Press, 1996.

Zhang Pingyi and Kang Yu. "Xianxian zhangzhuang tianzhujiao congjiaotangde fandong huodong ye dai dongnan renminde fan di ai guo yundong." In *Hebei wenshi cikan xuanji*, vol. 1. [Shijiazhuang] Hebei Renmin Chubanshe, 1980.

Zhang Ye. "Chinese NGOs: A Survey Report." In *Emerging Civil Society in the Asia Pacific Community: Nongovernmental Underpinnings of the Emerging Asia Pacific Regional Community*, edited by Tadashi Yamamoto. Singapore and Tokyo: Institute of Southeast Asian Studies and Japan Centre for International Exchange, 1995.

Index

Italicized page numbers refer to illustrations

activism, 58, 137; political, 112; in
  Taiwan, 145
activists: in Hong Kong, 143
Advisory Committee on Religious Freedom Abroad, 163n3
afterlife, 134. *See also* heaven
age, 97–98
Age of Exploration, 29
altar, *89*
Americans, 13, 127; Catholics, 2, 87. *See
  also* United States
Amnesty International, 84
anarchy, 127–28
ancestor worship, 4, 26, 55, 136
animosity: and solidarity, 60–63
anti-imperialism, 36
antimodernism, 95–99
apparitions: of the Virgin Mary, 91, 93–
  94
Archbishop of Tokyo, 41
arrests, 37, 43, 46, 163n4
asceticism, 47
Asia, 14; East, 127, 134; and underground Church support, 43
Asian Games, 41
Asia Watch, 43
associations, 12–14, 126, 132, 135; in

Hong Kong, 142; self-governed, 11–
  12; in Taiwan, 144–45. *See also*
  groups; organizations
Assumption, Feast of the, 1–2, *3*, 5, 8
atheism, 36, 114
Aurora University, 109
authoritarianism, 100, 129, 134
authority, 15, 22, 25–49, 58, 140–41; ecclesiastical, 15, 48–49, 62; hierarchical, 140; moral, 135; Vatican, 100
autonomy, 14, 36–37, 129, 133, 138; local, 54; religious, 101

Baodi County, 18, 66, 69–72
Baoding, 44, 91
baptism, 32, 86, 88–90; provisional, 57,
  88
Beijing, 2, 20, 41, 49, 71, 107–9, 114,
  132; Communist Party and, 34; seminaries, 104
Beijing University, 20
belligerence, 15, 22, 52–53, 64–65,
  140
Benedict XIV, 31
Benedict XV, 33, 86
Big Teaching (*xin da jiao*), 54–55, 64, 95,
  136